UNDERSTANDING DOCTORS

UNDERSTANDING DOCTORS

GETTING THE BEST HEALTH CARE

DR GILLIAN RICE

MICHAEL JOSEPH
LONDON

MICHAEL JOSEPH LTD

Published by the Penguin Group
27 Wrights Lane, London W8 5TZ, England
Viking Penguin Inc., 40 West 23rd Street, New York, New York 10010, USA
Penguin Books Australia Ltd, Ringwood, Victoria, Australia
Penguin Books Canada Ltd, 2801 John Street, Markham, Ontario, Canada L3R 1B4
Penguin Books (NZ) Ltd, 182–190 Wairau Road, Auckland 10, New Zealand

Penguin Books Ltd, Registered Offices: Harmondsworth, Middlesex, England

First published 1990

Copyright © Gillian Rice

Printed and bound in Great Britain by
Richard Clay Ltd, Bungay, Suffolk
Set in Monophoto Photina 11/13 pt
A CIP catalogue record for this book is available from the British Library

ISBN 0 7181 3436 2 paperback

Quotation on page 119 reproduced from *Children in Hospital – The Parents' View*, by
Ann Hales-Tooke, Priory Press, 1973, with the kind permission of Wayland Publishers
Ltd, 61 Western Road, Hove, BN3 1JD

In order to protect the identities of the doctors and patients interviewed in this book,
all their names have been changed.

For Andrew and Adrian, who started
the ball rolling

CONTENTS

ACKNOWLEDGEMENTS

MY THANKS GO to all the people who contributed to the production of this book, from its conception to publication.

To Drs Andrew Cunningham and Adrian Wilson of the Wellcome Unit for the History of Medicine, Cambridge University, who helped me to think critically and encouraged me to take up my pen and write again.

To my agent, Anthony Goff, for his efforts in getting the project off the ground, and to Susan Watt and Richenda Todd for their wise editorial input.

To all seventy-odd doctors and the many patients whom I interviewed. Most wished to remain anonymous so I cannot name them, but their willingness to discuss experiences and feelings so openly was crucial to my research.

Thanks also to the library staff at the Royal College of General Practitioners, to Kathy McGrath of the Medical Advisory Service, to Alison Scott of the Advertising Research Unit, University of Strathclyde and to Briony Brown and Kathy Vella who patiently waded through hundreds of hours of taped interviews and transcribed them for me.

Only with the tolerance of my former partners at the Paxton Green Health Centre in south London was I able to research and write the book whilst continuing to work in general practice. I am immensely grateful to them for this, especially to Dr Peter Roseveare who also read and commented on the manuscript.

Special thanks go to my husband Martin for his patience and support throughout the project.

FOREWORD

ON THE DAY I qualified as a doctor I looked ahead with excitement to my future career in medicine. The options were many; I could train for one of the hospital specialties, head into general practice, or follow an academic path concentrating on research and teaching. Since my teens I had been looking forward to 'working with people' so the academic road held no great attraction for me, and as my hospital-based training had biased me against general practice, it was with enthusiasm and ambition that I set out to make my career as a hospital specialist. I did well by normal standards, managing to secure some prestigious jobs and pass the necessary post-graduate exams, yet within three years of graduation I was sufficiently confused and disillusioned to find myself wondering if I had chosen the wrong career after all.

Why had I become so disenchanted? I thought long and hard about the question and was only able to answer it when I turned my back on medicine for a year, distancing myself from the hospital world that had previously engulfed me. When I looked objectively at my role as a doctor, the people that I had been so keen to work with seemed to have disappeared from sight. My days as a junior hospital doctor were busy and demanding, but the patients I cared for had least claim on my time. I had so many duties to fulfil that there was little time to stop and talk; I worried about their physical progress but had no time, and no training, to help me deal with the psychological and emotional aspects of their illness. I was a doctor, certainly, but the nature of my work conspired to separate me from the very people whom I had intended to be the focus of my attention.

After five years of training and three years of hospital

1

experience it was difficult for me to contemplate ending my career in medicine, but being a doctor was not what I had expected it to be, so I had grave doubts about staying in the profession. The one hope I clung to was that some other branch of medicine might prove more satisfying, so I changed direction and launched, somewhat anxiously, into general practice. I had every reason to feel apprehensive because I knew virtually nothing about a GP's life and work. Although in the 1970s about fifty per cent of medical graduates chose to go into general practice, my medical school curriculum devoted precious little time to the subject. Out of five years' training I spent a paltry two weeks in general practice; barely enough time to learn how to syringe ears and lance boils, let alone study the nature of GP–patient relationships, which is what I needed to know about to help me decide if general practice would prove more fulfilling than hospital work. Lacking any real understanding of the GP's role, my career switch was really little more than a blind grope in the dark, following a vague hunch that this path might lead me to a light at the end of the tunnel. Luckily for me, I was not disappointed. General practice provided a setting in which I was able to function as a doctor in the way I had always intended, and, as a result, I discovered the kind of job satisfaction which I had begun to fear that medicine could never give me.

On moving from a hospital environment into general practice I was amazed to find just how greatly my work changed. I was still a doctor but the role I fulfilled for patients was very different. As a junior in hospitals, practical tasks and clerical duties were often the focus of my attention rather than the people under my care. I had so little time to spend with patients that for many I'm sure I was little more than the white-coated figure who stopped briefly by the end of their bed each day. As a GP, although I was involved just as much with diagnosing and treating disease, I was able to deal with this part of my work without losing sight of the patients. I realised that I could be a confidante, counsellor and friend as well as the body-healer I had tried to be in hospital.

Although I felt myself to be quite a different doctor as a GP than I had been as a hospital junior I rapidly became aware that to some patients all doctors were the same. Many people seem to have a set idea of a doctor's function, and an equally immutable image of their own role as a patient. These patients saw me as a professional stereotype and the way they related to me was predetermined by their notion of what was 'acceptable' patient behaviour.

I began to realise how intimidated some people are by doctors – or at least by the image of doctors they have grown up with and come to accept. Their belief in the doctor as some kind of superior being makes it difficult for them to communicate effectively, and the problem is further compounded when the doctor accepts this demigod role and remains distanced from the person he is trying to treat. No doubt some doctors enjoy being put on a pedestal but I find it a rather lonely and uncomfortable position. I don't believe it can benefit patients either, for when they have unrealistic expectations of a doctor they will often persist in wanting a magic cure rather than accepting more practical ways of dealing with their problems.

Having discovered both the limitations and the potential of my role as a doctor in hospital and in general practice, I was motivated to write this book for several reasons. Firstly, I felt guilty about spending so little time with my hospital patients and wanted them to know that this was not the result of indifference on my part, but was due more to the demands and pressures to which housemen and other junior doctors are subjected. Secondly, I feel strongly that the myths about doctors which mask our human qualities frighten and inhibit many patients. By dismantling such myths and showing doctors as they really are, I hope it will be easier for people to communicate and build satisfying relationships with them. Thirdly (and most selfishly), I wanted to free myself and other doctors from the burden of unrealistic expectations which are so often heaped upon us. If this book does anything to break down barriers between doctors and patients, as I hope it will, it should be of some benefit to us all.

CHAPTER 1

MYTHS AND MISCONCEPTIONS

As a healthy youngster I was lucky enough to need little medical attention during my childhood and teens. I must have come into contact with our local GP now and again but the meetings were so brief and infrequent that they left no lasting impression on me. Yet by the time I left school something had sufficiently impressed me about the medical profession to make me decide to join their ranks and become a doctor.

I had no relatives who were doctors, nor any close family friends who gave me insight into the profession. Instead, my image of the medical world was shaped by what I read in books and magazines, and by early medical 'soaps', like *Dr Kildare* and *Emergency Ward 10*, that I saw on television. All these sources painted doctors as white-coated heroes, with their work a mixture of drama, tragedy and joy. I quickly accepted this romanticised image of doctors as reality, for nothing in my personal experience served to contradict what I gleaned about them through the media. Like many other people I came to view doctors as a special breed, quite different from the rest of us ordinary mortals. Their apparent wisdom and omniscience made them a group to be respected and revered.

Once I was medically qualified myself, I began to realise how difficult it was to live up to this idealised image of 'The Doctor'. On the other hand, I also discovered from my contact with patients how deeply ingrained the notion of doctor-as-hero is in our society. Although people may criticise individual doctors for failings such as ineptitude, arrogance or indifference, this does not stop many believing the generalisation that 'good' doctors are superhuman as well as saintly. There is also a common assumption that every member of the medical profession is meant to play exactly the same role for patients – a blend of curing, counselling and caring – and that any doctor who does not is failing his patients.

Although when I began my medical training I, too, believed that all doctors fitted the same mould and were destined to serve patients in the same way, my experience as a hospital junior and GP has convinced me otherwise. In the years since graduation, I have watched friends and colleagues carve out their careers in general practice and hospital medicine, the latter group struggling through difficult times on the lowest rungs of the hospital ladder in the hope of one day winning a coveted consultant post. As they climb up the hospital hierarchy their duties change, and the kind of contact they have with patients changes too. Listening to them describe the nature of their work, I realise how much they have altered as doctors since the days when we were housemen together. They have not changed as people, but career demands mean that they view patients in a different way, and function differently in their doctor role.

So, when I analysed my own experiences and the changes evident in my medical friends, I realised how greatly certain circumstances influenced the relationships that each of us had with patients. To outsiders we might appear as an amorphous group labelled 'Doctors', but from within I was aware of the distinct roles we performed for patients, according to our workplace (for example hospital or general practice) and our position within the medical hierarchy.

The roles that doctors play also vary according to the problems they find themselves dealing with. This is partly a result of conscious decision-making: no doctor is likely to adopt the same attitude to a recently bereaved widow as to a plumber with back pain, for they will recognise their differing needs and approach each one accordingly. Unconscious forces also come into play, modifying the doctor's response to a patient. Human feelings, from embarrassment and fear to grief and anger, are not exclusive to patients, but doctors often feel ambivalent about revealing their emotions, fearful that their professional strength may be diminished by exposure of their human selves.

However well hidden they may be, those same feelings *do* exist, and they have a significant influence on the way doctors and patients relate to one another.

Why then is this a side of doctors about which most people know so little? The reasons are complex, but an important factor is the tendency of doctors to maintain a certain distance between themselves and the people they treat. Until now this has helped to reinforce their therapeutic power; just as a tribesman's belief in the witch doctor's magic may have enhanced the potency of his medicines, so Western physicians have long used their authority and status in a similar way, knowing that a patient's faith and trust in the doctor is helpful in securing a successful outcome to their treatment. But doctors can no longer rely on being the hallowed figures of society they once were, for in the present climate of growing health awareness many people are not prepared to take their word as gospel.

As a patient you may have learnt a lot about your body and health from television, books and magazines, and so may challenge your doctor's diagnoses, question his advice, and reject his orthodox treatments in favour of alternative therapies more than your parents or grandparents would ever have dared to do. You may well feel unhappy playing passive patient to a directive doctor, wanting instead a relationship in which you are given more information and explanation, and a greater say in decisions concerning your medical treatment. People often marvel at continuing advances in medical research and technology, but are less enthusiastic about the effects that high-tech medicine has on doctors' bedside manner. They appreciate the benefits of current medical knowledge and new therapeutic techniques, but still lament the passing of the old-style family doctor, whose personal attention and caring attitude were much appreciated. What many patients seem to want is a partnership with their doctor in which they are treated as a thinking, feeling human being, not as a malfunctioning machine.

Is such a partnership possible? Perhaps, as long as doctors learn to understand more fully the layman's experience of illness and all the feelings it evokes. If they can achieve that, and can communicate their empathy to patients, doctors will go a long way to providing the 'human' approach that many people want. What their efforts will not produce is a partnership in which free and open dialogue flourishes because both partners feel able to communicate on a personal as well as a professional level.

To achieve this, the understanding between doctor and patient must be more than one-way, but until now it has been hard for patients to reciprocate such an effort on the doctor's part. People generally know little about the attitudes, feelings and experiences of men and women in the medical profession, and so have had little hope of 'knowing' their doctor in a meaningful way. It has been difficult for them to see him as anything but a professional stereotype – a competent, caring doctor perhaps, but not a human being whose feelings and behaviour are influenced by people and events. This situation can be remedied though; if patients are given more insight into the medical world (as this book attempts to provide), they will be better able to understand and influence their relationships with doctors.

There is a real need to foster this kind of mutual understanding because the stereotyped image of doctors, which has survived through many centuries, has set them apart from the rest of society; around it has evolved a myth that doctors are demigods, imbued with special skills and wisdom and unfettered by human failings and weaknesses. The image has become so entrenched in our culture that although the public is increasingly well informed about medical matters, their understanding of the doctors who treat them is based largely on myth and fantasy. They have no real knowledge of the medical world and how it affects doctors in their working lives. People see only the professional 'mask' of doctors – the image they present both consciously and unconsciously to their patients – and behind that much else is hidden.

Why are doctors enshrouded by this cloak of mystery? Undoubtedly part of the reason lies in the knowledge and skills they acquire, tools with which they can explore the complexities of body and mind. They make sense of signs and symptoms which the layman cannot fathom. They can battle with disease, halt illness in its tracks and even snatch victims from the clutches of death. Using specially trained senses and a range of instruments from the simple to the sophisticated, they can 'see' inside the body and root out hidden problems. They use knowledge as a key to unlock the body's mysteries – an awesome feat to those who cannot force the lock themselves.

The nature of medical training has also contributed to the perception of doctors as a breed apart, for it encourages them to become guarded and aloof. Fierce competition for entry into medical school means that students who win a place are usually those already accustomed to academic success. Fear of failure encourages rivalry amongst them, and the weapon of ridicule commonly used by their teachers makes them uncertain and defensive about their knowledge and skills.

I remember one incident during my medical school training when I stood with a group of fellow students around a patient's bed, being taught by a sharp-tongued and short-tempered consultant. Taking no account of our junior status, the consultant proceeded to berate one particularly nervous student for his ignorance, humiliating him in front of his peers and the patient. As a result of experiences like this, many medical students develop a façade of brash confidence to hide the anxieties that lurk within. Qualifying as a doctor only hardens this shell, for the pressure to succeed is then even greater. Determination and drive may help doctors succeed in the medical rat race but it can also dull their concern for others. Moulded in this way, they become distanced not only from their colleagues, but also from the patients in need of their care.

Doctors' remoteness is not due solely to professional rivalry; it is also a reaction to the stress of the job. Caring for patients can be emotionally draining and many doctors find it easier to suppress their feelings than confront them. With their emotions in check they can put on a convincing display of stoicism and strength; they can deal with patients' emotions while protecting their own behind a wall of apparent invulnerability. Such machismo undoubtedly hides many of doctors' human frailties, and in so doing, adds to their mystique in society's eyes.

While the medical profession has perched safely on its pedestal, content to remain distanced from the lay public, some patients have continued to trust and respect doctors, but others have rejected our claims to medical authority and a special place in

8

society. In the past doctors were highly regarded not because they could influence the course of disease – very often they were powerless to do so – but because people believed they had special knowledge, a vocation to serve, and a commitment to confidentiality and human care which gave them a 'priestly' role in the community. As science and technology have enabled doctors to prevent, control and cure more illness, for many people medicine has become increasingly enigmatic and doctors even more awesome than before. For others, advances in medicine have raised expectations so greatly that they are unwilling to tolerate any degree of ill health, and think that doctors who can't provide an instant cure for their every ailment are failing them dismally. Indeed, for a few people technology has become the master and the doctor merely its servant; reared in a society which is, in some ways at least, more egalitarian, and in which the consumer rules, a minority of people seem to view doctors with contempt.

I recently heard a disillusioned GP lament that 'there are only two kinds of patients – those who revere us and put us on a pedestal, and the rest who treat us like biological tradesmen'. Although a rather cynical view, it is one that I can sympathise with to an extent. I think many people do expect a doctor to be a kind of medical Superman – strong, dependable, and able to banish every ailment in a flash – while a few disillusioned patients see the profession, and especially GPs, as little more than a bunch of medical mechanics whose job it is to provide tuning, servicing and breakdown repairs on demand. Although the latter group have disentangled themselves from one myth, they have ensnared themselves in another, and in the process have come no closer to finding out what really makes doctors tick.

But does it matter if you don't understand your doctor, and cannot easily relate to him as a person as well as a professional? After all, few people know much about their bank manager, accountant or solicitor, yet may be perfectly content with the services they provide. You will probably be happy with a bank manager if he's sympathetic to your financial needs, and feel satisfied with a solicitor so long as your legal affairs are handled well. Personal rapport between you isn't essential for

9

the professional to do his job, or for you to be satisfied with his service.

Not so with a doctor; when people are ill they often go to him in search of sympathy, understanding and reassurance, and rarely come away satisfied if he doesn't cater to their emotional needs as well as their physical ailments. Psychological and emotional factors play such an important part in illness that if a doctor fails to communicate with a patient on a human level, exploring and resolving emotions like fear, anger or bitterness, which may be bubbling away beneath the surface, he may be frustrated in his attempts to make them well. Likewise, it is important for people to have some regard for their doctor as another human being if they want to get the most caring service from him. Doctors, just like everyone else, feel more inclined to make an effort for people who show their appreciation.

For most people it is not enough for a doctor to be a competent professional; he must also show himself to be a sensitive human being, so that they can share with him the emotional issues which they experience as an integral part of any illness. Perhaps it seems melodramatic to attach such importance to the human bond linking doctor and patient. If you visit your doctor only for holiday vaccinations or repeat prescriptions of the Pill, you may not feel any need for deep and intuitive understanding on his part. In these situations professional competence and convenient access to the doctor may be all you require. Unfortunately, few problems brought to doctors are so easily dealt with. Many do have an emotional or psychological basis, or repercussions of that kind, which must be acknowledged by the doctor if the patient is to leave feeling satisfied. For most people, the doctor's professional expertise is not enough; they also need his warmth and understanding, for this provides an emotional tonic which revives the parts that ordinary drugs cannot reach.

The difficulty for patients trying to convey their need for human empathy, and for doctors attempting to satisfy it, is that the relationship between them is undoubtedly different from one between any other professional and client, so they find themselves without a clear set of rules to dictate what they can give to, and take from, one another. The mystique which surrounds doctors makes it difficult for people to accept them as ordinary human beings, yet they must credit doctors with human emotions if they hope to receive that sort of understanding from them. As we'll see in later chapters, doctors, too, find themselves caught in a net of conflicting anxieties; they fear the loss of their authority if they are seen to be ordinary and human, yet would welcome a respite from demands heaped upon them as a result of myths they have failed to dispel. Both patients and doctors are caught in a dilemma, uncertain how much emotional intimacy they can share without endangering the safe structure of the 'professional relationship'.

Doctors are increasingly aware that to give a better service to patients they must concentrate on *people*, not merely the illnesses they present. But for meaningful rapport between doctors and patients this kind of understanding must flow both ways. While the public's knowledge of the medical profession is based on myth, not reality, they will never make sense of their relationships with doctors. People's ignorance about the medical world paves the way for misunderstanding; their misguided expectations lead to disappointment and discontent.

Part of the problem for the man in the street is that he has never really been given an opportunity to see inside the medical world. Only doctors themselves can draw back the curtains to reveal what goes on behind the scenes, but the profession has shown little inclination to do so. It seems to behave like an anxious theatre company, keen to keep the audience firmly in their seats, for fear that a view of reality backstage would diminish the credibility of the actors' performance.

The profession's silence has helped to perpetuate the idealised image of doctors which so many people believe. We have avoided showing people the inner sanctums of our world, frightened that familiarity might invite contempt to creep in. Some doctors would prefer to play safe and preserve the existing mystique, but I'm convinced it is time for the profession to take a risk, and let people see what a doctor's world is really like. They need to understand the hierarchy and the hard work, the politics and the pressures, our experiences and our emotions, for all of those shape the way we interact with patients. Only then will people recognise the human side of doctors, and be able to

11

make sense of the way they behave. The reality may shatter a few illusions, but that is surely a small price to pay if it helps to dismantle the myths and misconceptions which currently hold doctors and patients apart.

I hope this book will help people think beyond a single image of 'the doctor', for it is important to understand the subdivisions of the medical profession. I will describe in detail the worlds of three broad categories of doctors: housemen, consultants and general practitioners, and realise that by concentrating on the most junior and senior of the hospital grades, and on GPs, I will give scant attention to the middle ranks of hospital doctors and to some of the other community-based medical specialties. My aim though, is not to provide an exhaustive review of the profession, grade by grade, and specialty by specialty, but rather to give a general idea of how a doctor's position in the medical hierarchy, and his placement in hospital or the community, affects his view of patients and of the role he is meant to play for them.

Breaking down the generalised 'doctor role' into cameos played by GPs, housemen and consultants cannot explain the myriad subtleties of any individual relationship between a doctor and a patient; the personalities involved naturally produce a unique bond which will be different from that between any other doctor and patient. But an attempt to dissolve the falsely unified image of 'The Doctor' can help people get closer to *real* doctors, human beings whose instinctive thoughts, behaviour and reactions are tempered in different ways by the demands of their specific medical job.

As I've mentioned, doctors are not only influenced by their rank and work setting, but also by the nature of the problems they have to deal with. For example, doctors feel quite differently about pregnancy and childbirth, death and dying, acute illness, chronic illness and sick children; by examining their response to patients in these categories I hope to show that the doctor–patient relationship is not immutable in its form, but is something which can change throughout a person's life and will, in part, be determined by the condition which necessitates the doctor's help.

I've said that I will highlight the differences between doctors, and the variation in their relationships with patients, but there is, in addition, much common ground among doctors, whatever our grade or specialty, and wherever we work. We all experience a very similar training which exerts a powerful influence on our view of patients, illness and health; by changing our perception of the body and mind it also separates us from the general public.

We enter medical school at seventeen or eighteen, differentiated from most other teenagers only by the high academic standards we have had to achieve to be selected for medical training, but we emerge at the end of a five- or six-year course moulded into doctors, with knowledge and experience which sets us apart from the layman. The peculiar nature of this training explains a good deal about doctors' view of themselves and of their role in society, and is responsible for much of the distance between doctors and the people they treat. In the final chapter I will therefore focus on certain aspects of medical training, to try and help readers understand the way it influences doctors' attitudes, and to point out the areas in which changes need to be made for the benefit of both patients and their doctors.

I know that, as a doctor, I enjoy a privileged position in British society, but I am also aware that such a position is tenuous and will be eroded if people's dissatisfaction with the medical profession grows. I welcome my patients' respect if they think I earn it through my knowledge, experience, or commitment to them and their care, but to be revered for god-like attributes I do not possess, and on the basis of expectations I cannot live up to, makes me feel uncomfortable for two reasons. Firstly, if I perpetuate the myth, I am guilty of being an impostor, a fraud; and secondly, there is every chance I will fail to live up to the idealised image and so will be rejected by disappointed and disillusioned patients.

People have every right to expect doctors to be knowledgeable, competent and caring. They should be confident of doctors' willingness to explain, inform and reassure. We should make decisions and shoulder uncertainty for patients when they want us to, but be prepared to share decisions and doubts when they wish to play a greater part in their own medical management.

13

While it is reasonable for patients to expect a service incorporating all these elements, I think it is dangerous, both for them and for doctors, to cling to myths about the medical profession which encourage unrealistic expectations and a belief in the doctor as a superhuman figure. The profession has never actively discouraged such myths, and, as a result, doctors have struggled to live up to an idealised image of themselves. Such an endeavour takes its toll on many and contributes to the increased incidence of suicide, alcohol abuse and psychiatric illness amongst doctors. Hardly the stuff that heroes are made of.

By painting a true-to-life picture of the working world of doctors, I want to help bridge the gap between the medical profession and the public. Doctors are rightly under pressure to consider patients more as thinking, feeling human beings; this book prompts readers to view doctors in a similar light. Not primarily for their benefit, but for your own, because to get the best out of your dealings with doctors you need to know more about them and how they relate to you as a patient. When you understand more about doctors you will be better able to make sure *they* understand *you* too.

CHAPTER 2

THE HOUSEMAN

EVERY YEAR ON the first day of August, newly qualified doctors all over Great Britain hover nervously at the entrance to hospital wards. With their medical degree course successfully completed, they must now spend twelve months in a kind of hospital apprenticeship in order to become fully qualified. The year is split into two six-month 'housejobs', one on a medical, and the other on a surgical 'firm'. The experience gained by doctors during this inaugural year varies tremendously, depending on the area in which they work, the size and type of hospital, and the nature of the patients' problems on their particular wards. One factor remains the same for all housemen though: their position at the very bottom of the medical hierarchy.

As a ward patient, curious yet apprehensive about the hospital environment in which you find yourself, you will probably have little idea of just how petrified that new houseman is. With his newly acquired 'Dr' name badge proudly adorning his starched white coat, and his pockets displaying an impressive range of medical books and instruments, he may seem every bit the confident young doctor. In reality he is probably a nervous wreck, wondering if he will be able to cope with the re-sponsibility of being a 'real' doctor.

For a naïve young houseman, the obstacles littering the hospital career path appear as no more than a dim shadow on the horizon. As they begin their ascent of the hospital hierarchy, most housemen aren't aware of the difficulties they will face in trying to reach the summit, and even if they were, other more immediate worries are far more likely to concern them. During your first few weeks on the wards you worry about things like putting 'drips' into veins, missing fractures on skull X-rays, treating asthmatic attacks and heart failure, 'clerking' ten patients a day, having results ready for the week's big ward round, remembering the right drugs, and the right doses, for every condition you're faced with, and whether you'll make a fool of yourself in front of your consultant. For weeks you're on tenterhooks, plagued by the conviction that your first big blunder is just around the corner. Little do patients realise that the doctor who keeps vanishing and reappearing is sneaking a look at the medical manuals to make sure that what he's doing is correct! As in few other jobs, people's lives or well-being can be jeopardised by your mistakes, so you can't even reason with yourself that you'll learn by trial and error – unless you're prepared for the trial to be in a court of law, with charges of negligence brought against you.

During those first few weeks of nail-biting anxiety every houseman will, in theory, be supported and supervised by the more senior doctors working with him. Unfortunately, theory and practice sometimes bear little resemblance. The 'firm' the houseman works for may consist of only himself and the consultant, or include numerous other doctors at various grades. Most can be summoned by a bleep, but a houseman will often be reluctant to call for advice, fearing that he will be chided for not managing alone. That fear is usually unfounded but the lessons of medical school, where ignorance is ridiculed and an air of capability much admired, leaves a powerful imprint on the minds of newly qualified doctors and makes them frightened to admit their inexperience and need for instruction. Most will find a way round the problem; they scuttle off and ask another junior doctor for help, delve into *The Houseman's Handbook* in search of sound advice, or perhaps swallow their pride after all, and ask someone more senior to come to their rescue. Serious errors are thankfully few and far between, but as all of us can remember our own early gaffes, we quietly tell our families that hospitals are to be avoided when the year's new brood of housemen are let loose on the wards!

Television, books and films have made the haggard and weary houseman a well-recognised figure, but even allowing for a liberal use of artistic licence and journalistic colour, the popular portrayal of a junior doctor is often disturbingly close to the truth. The houseman's routine day, stretching from eight or nine in the morning to five or six at night, may be no longer than most people's, but the nights 'on call' which they are also obliged to work bring their weekly workload up to anything between 70 and 110 hours. In February 1989 a Bill to reduce junior doctors' hours received an unopposed second reading in the House of Lords but was defeated immediately when it went to the Commons, so there seems no end in sight to the arduous workload these doctors must endure.

Nightwork is organised according to rotas which vary from hospital to hospital, but a 'one-in-three' or 'one-in-four' rota is common for housejobs. The one-in-three rota, for example, means that in addition to a five-day working week the house-man will be on duty every third night and every third weekend. If he is 'first on call' for the night he will have been dealing with all the emergency medical or surgical admissions since nine a.m. and will continue to do so until nine o'clock the following morning – a duty known in England and Wales as being 'on take' or in Scotland as 'waiting'. As the 'second on call' he'll be responsible for patients who are already on the wards, rather than the new admissions. A weekend 'on call' usually stretches over a 48-hour period, from early on Saturday until Monday morning, and is always followed by a full working day which ends on Monday evening. Some jobs are even tougher, requiring the houseman to work a horrendous 80-hour haul, from Friday morning right the way through to Monday evening, whenever they are on call for the weekend.

During any on-call duty, sleep is precious and usually inter-rupted; the houseman may get to bed before midnight, but the chances of him staying there until morning are remote. It's not uncommon to be woken three or four times during the night and each task can take anything from ten minutes to an hour to deal with, even longer if it involves admitting and treating a seriously ill patient. There is no shift system which ensures that these two or three days on duty are followed by a few days off work; the on-call responsibilities may finish on Monday morning but routine duties continue as usual until the end of the day when the houseman collapses in a heap and tries to recuperate with a solid night's sleep.

It's obviously a system which puts enormous strain on housemen and which is unfair both to them and to patients. Most doctors' reserves of tolerance and compassion are at rock bottom when they've been dragged out of bed at five a.m., having only been back between the sheets for half an hour since the last call. The patient therefore has to face a dopey, short-tempered doctor, whose bedside manner didn't make it out of bed at all, and whose number-one priority is getting back to sleep as quickly as possible. Even more worrying is the fact that tiredness can make the houseman unsafe as well as unsympathetic, for all history-taking and physical examination tends to be perfunctory when you're half asleep and functioning on auto-pilot.

Many doctors, if pressed, will admit to at least one near-disaster caused by fatigue, and a friend once told me about his close shave. He'd been up most of the night admitting emergency cases, and had finally sent the last one to the ward. The patient struck him as a rather taciturn man, complaining of some niggling abdominal pain. It didn't seem serious but it was easier to admit him than try and find him transport home, so the man went to the ward for 'observation' and my friend went thankfully back to his room to sleep.

As he drifted into unconsciousness, the man's dull gaze and uncommunicative manner floated tantalisingly in and out of his mind, leaving him with a vague feeling of unease. A moment of ghastly realisation jolted him awake, whereupon he rushed up to the ward and found the man apparently snoring peacefully. He jabbed the patient's thumb with a pin (causing not a flicker of response), tested a drop of blood for sugar, and noted the alarmingly high result with a mixture of horror and relief. The man was obviously diabetic and his laconic speech had been due to incipient coma. With all dopiness now banished by a huge surge of adrenalin, my friend did the necessary and by morning the man was out of danger. He knew he had initially failed to make a correct diagnosis because he was too tired to think, or even really care, about what was wrong. Luckily for him, and the patient, in that twilight period before deep sleep came his brain made sense of the signs he had at first ignored. Most incidents of this kind probably never come to light, but I'm sure mistakes are made and patients sometimes suffer because of the intolerably long hours many junior doctors have to work.

It's a sad fact that until the medical manpower problem in this country is resolved there will undoubtedly continue to be doctors and patients who escape disaster by a whisker, and perhaps a few who don't escape at all.

Considering their long hours of work, junior doctors are by no means overpaid. The present system, which gives them a basic salary for a 40-hour week, plus overtime payments for their extra hours on duty, was negotiated in the mid-1970s when junior hospital staff took unofficial industrial action in support of their claim for better pay and conditions. These 'extra' hours are, in fact, compulsory, yet paid at only 38 per cent of the standard rate; little wonder then that junior doctors working 50 to 60 hours on call each week, and being paid only a third of their normal rate for doing so, often feel hard done by. What's more surprising is that they put up with it, but agitators among the ranks tend to be unpopular with consultants, so most junior doctors prefer to toe the line, rather than put their careers at risk by fighting for a better deal.

It's eight years now since I was a houseman but I have very clear memories of the highs and lows of those 12 months. The pride I felt when coping with serious medical problems was very real, as was my enjoyment of caring for patients. The plus side of the job was, however, often soured by exhaustion and resentment at the never-ending demands heaped upon me. I knew I had reached rock bottom one night when I was on call and was summoned from bed for the third time to see a patient in Casualty. As I dragged myself along the hospital corridors, fatigue and self-pity overcame me and I fled into a Ladies' toilet to sob my heart out. A night cleaner found me there a few minutes later and I remember hiding my tear-stained face in embarrassment, feeling that I must be failing as a doctor if I couldn't cope with the gruelling workload which seemed to be the norm.

When I set out to write this book I knew that my own recollections couldn't be taken as a blueprint for all other doctors doing the job. I had a sneaking suspicion though, that things now are much the same as they were during my days as a junior in hospitals, and the many housemen I spoke to around Britain confirmed that impression. They also brought back to me the fears and frustrations of the job, and made it clear how the attitude of the more senior doctors they worked with greatly coloured their enjoyment of the year.

Dr Graham Hunt was a tall, slim and amiable young man in his mid-twenties, coming to the end of his houseman year in a London teaching hospital:

‘I survived so you can too’

When I started I found the responsibility very difficult. Suddenly, on my first night on call, I was looking after three wards of surgical patients with a registrar at the end of a telephone somewhere and I just had to get on with it. I got very irritable. I was shit scared basically, didn't know what I was doing, that's what made me irritable. The attitude from other doctors was 'I did it and I survived so you can jolly well survive too'. I felt I couldn't possibly admit defeat and phone the registrar and have him say, 'Really, it's very simple.'

Dr Helen Badcock, a houseman at a small local hospital in Kent, was also nearing the end of her housejobs when we met. Her broad face and dark-brown eyes exuded warmth and honesty. Her memories of the early part of housejobs echoed those of Graham Hunt:

‘The first month was just awful’

The first month of being a houseman was just awful, awful. If I was on take I used to go to bed thinking, Something's going to happen and I haven't done this or that – very, very worried about everything. But gradually you become more confident and the anxiety goes away.

When I asked Helen if she ever felt that too much was being demanded of her as a houseman, she pinpointed the kind of days when the pressure seemed to mount up to an unbearable level:

If I'm tired and busy, if I'm being hassled in a lot of directions, if someone's ill on the ward and I'm supposed to be in Casualty but the nurses want me to talk to some relatives, if I haven't had supper and I missed my sleep last night, I just think, Why do I have to do this? I start to feel I'm not enjoying it, I'm not getting many rewards for it, and I'm going to have to do it for the rest of my life. Then I think I'm not doing it as well as I should do and everything gets on top of me. But you just have to cope and get over it.

Dr Mark Shearing struck me as unnaturally confident for a 24-year-old houseman. The account he gave of his first year on the wards left me feeling that I'd listened to an unflappable middle-aged physician rather than a young, inexperienced doctor. He claimed not to have been dogged by the early anxieties which affected most of his peers and he appeared to have been luckier than many of the other housemen in the level of support afforded to him at the start of his housejobs:

'I've been very lucky'

I had close liaison with the consultants in my first housejob. I had no registrar cover when I was on call, so if I wanted help I had to ring the consultants but they were very helpful and would come in. They never told me off for asking something. If it was a bloody stupid question they'd say 'You might've worked that out for yourself' but they were never angry.

I've been very lucky. I seem to get quite a few hours' sleep at night, even when I'm on take. I don't actually find work stressful. You're providing a service. You're doing a job and you have to accept that people get ill at all times of the day and night and it's not their fault that you happen to be hard pushed.

Dr Tessa Collins was three months into her first housejob at a modern district general hospital in North Wales. She had joined the army while still a medical student because of the future job security it offered her. As we chatted in the hospital flat which she shared with a girlfriend from medical school, she spoke eagerly, as if sharing a burdensome secret:

'I don't think medical school prepares you for being a houseman'

Some aspects of the job I've liked and some I've hated. Some of it's come as a bit of a shock really. I don't think medical school prepares you particularly well for being a houseman.

21

I've found it harder to cope with being on call than I thought I would. I'm not too bad during the night because I find I get a kind of second wind which helps me carry on, but the next day I'm really flagging. It definitely affects my concentration and I find I'm really slow. It affects your patience too. You lose your temper over something really trivial which wouldn't have provoked you normally, but it's different when you're tired.

There was a period in the first few weeks of the job, and from talking to the others it seems we all went through it, when we coped all right. But then the lack of sleep caught up with us and everybody went through a terrible dark depression. We're just coming out of it now and starting to cope again. It certainly affected me like that. I felt really down at one stage.

People are affected quite a lot by the stresses of the job. I know of several colleagues who've burst into tears on a ward round. And I did the same thing the other night. I had patients to clerk, couldn't get round to doing the six o'clock IV [intravenous] drugs until half-past nine and then the registrar sent me off to the emergency drug cupboard to get something just when I was in the middle of doing something else. It was a silly reason to cry, but I just felt utterly exasperated.

Research carried out in England and America confirms this anecdotal evidence of the stress suffered by housemen. Some North American authors cite reported rates for depression of at least 33 per cent. A recent study in Sheffield was precipitated by the reaction of staff to the suicides of two junior house officers. It showed that amongst the 170 housemen questioned, levels of stress were higher than in other occupational groups, and 28 per cent of the group showed evidence of depression. The young doctors reported 'overwork' as being the most stressful aspect of their jobs, followed by 'talking to distressed relatives', 'effects on personal life' and 'serious treatment failures'. Interestingly, the number of hours worked were not related to stress levels (as scored by the study) but lack of sleep, problems adjusting to sleep patterns, and an inadequate diet were. Housemen in teaching hospitals seem to experience more stress than those in non-teaching hospitals, possibly because of the more competitive atmosphere in which they work, and because these young doctors are often the brightest or most ambitious of their year, with higher expectations of themselves than the average medical student.[1]

Although most doctors seem to remember their houseman year as an exhausting and stressful time, many nevertheless regard it as a necessary initiation into the world of medicine and think that those who complain simply aren't tough enough for the job. Some consultants pooh-pooh the moans of their juniors, barking dismissively that 'things were *much* worse in my day . . .' Few of us would dispute that, yet instead of making them sympathetic to the young doctors of today their experiences appear to have encouraged them to view housejobs as a trial of endurance which only the strongest (and, in their eyes, the best) doctors survive. There is undoubtedly a tendency within the profession to regard the resilient as 'good' doctors and the distressed as 'poor' ones. This attitude is bred into us from our formative days as medical students when our teachers are consultants (the survivors in a demanding and, at times, ruthlessly competitive hospital world), and registrars or senior registrars who are striving to emulate the success of their bosses.

With role models like these, it's hardly surprising that students don't see sensitivity as a personal attribute to nurture, and may later feel disdainful of doctors who have difficulty coping with the job. Ironically, the supposedly caring profession of medicine breeds doctors who exhibit precious little care for one another.

Housemen grappling with the duties and responsibilities of the first year in hospital often cite their relationships with consultants and other doctors on the firm as a factor which greatly influences job satisfaction. In part this reflects their need to have ready and willing support close at hand, but it also indicates a strong desire for approval and appreciation. Rightly or wrongly, the houseman looks to his seniors, not his patients, for a judgement on his performance, so a good relationship with the former is of paramount importance to his self-esteem.

1. Firth-Cozens, J., 'Emotional distress in junior house officers', *British Medical Journal*, 1987; vol. 295, pp. 533–6.

'They were very supportive'

DR HELEN BADCOCK: They were very supportive, always there, very interested in the patients and what you thought about them. They wanted you to do the job properly and they wanted it done in a kind of formal way so you had to know all the patients and the examination findings, but there were never any hassles if you hadn't done something or couldn't have done it, and because of that I know I tried especially hard to do it well. In my second housejob I tried very hard to do things well, not because I admired the consultant, but because I disliked him and because I didn't want him to have any 'getback' at me if he didn't like me. I wanted to do it well for the wrong reasons.

'He just used to bark'

DR GRAHAM HUNT: There was me and a senior registrar who was what I call very 'consultoid'. He just used to stand there and bark the orders out and didn't actually give me any help. That was difficult. It's nice to have someone, a registrar or SHO, who's more your age group and can remember being a houseman, and remember all the hassle.

'They made you feel part of the team'

DR MARK SHEARING: My consultants were very supportive. They were interested in you not only as a houseman but as a person and they made you feel part of the team. They asked your opinion – maybe they didn't take any notice of it, but they asked, and that's important because you then feel you can contribute something.

It's hardly surprising that patients have little influence on the houseman's enjoyment of his job, since only a minimal part of his day is spent dealing with them directly. It's true that most of his work is in some way connected with patients, but time spent investigating, treating or monitoring someone's illness isn't necessarily time spent at their bedside. Many of the houseman's duties, in fact, require no face-to-face contact with patients at all: arranging X-rays, blood tests and other investigations, plus penning the innumerable forms which are needed to authorise them, updating information in patients' notes, arranging operating lists and helping the surgeon in theatre, liaising with GPs, social workers, and other health professionals, chasing up results of tests, and a variety of menial tasks too numerous to mention. All of it forms part of a process which aims to restore patients to health, but a process which makes so many demands on housemen that they frequently feel there is no time to sit and talk with the actual people their work revolves around.

I know that one of my consultants regarded me as a very competent houseman because I could deal efficiently with all these tasks, but it took a patient to point out the cost of such 'efficiency' to him (and other patients). As I hurried past this elderly man's bed one day on my way to the X-ray department he looked up from his newspaper and said, 'I always know when you're around, Dr Rice, because I hear you galloping in and out of the ward like a racehorse.' He didn't need to add that all my rushed to-ing and fro-ing made it impossible for him to catch me for even a brief word.

The housemen's workload is undoubtedly one cause for patients seeing so little of them. Another, more disturbing, reason is the tendency of medical schools to teach students how to treat disease, rather than people affected by disease. Emphasis is placed not on knowing the patient, but on knowing what is wrong with him. Would-be doctors learn in detail about the drugs and surgical techniques which are used in treatment, but medical training pays scant attention to the psychological and emotional aspects of illness, let alone teaches students how to influence them through their relationships with patients.

As a result, junior doctors arrive on the wards brimming with factual knowledge but painfully lacking in communication skills. Personality overcomes these deficiencies for some; the gregarious put patients at ease with their natural ebullience and humour, while the empathetic win confidence through genuine concern. Many, however, remain as awkward with patients as an acned teenager with his first date. Erica Freeman, a 45-year-old housewife in hospital to have a breast removed because of cancer, was none too complimentary about the houseman she'd encountered:

'He looked young and inexperienced'

I'm really depressed about having the breast off. I keep worrying that my husband won't find me attractive any more, that he'll go off and have an affair with someone. When the houseman first came to see me he certainly didn't help me feel any better. He looked young and inexperienced and behaved that way too. When I mentioned my worries he just looked uncomfortable and said, 'Oh, I'm sure you've nothing to fear,' and changed the subject.

Erica's experience is by no means unusual. Such lack of ease in relating to patients, coupled with the belief that a doctor's primary role is to diagnose and treat rather than care and support, means that some housemen shy away from spending time with patients, even when their job is quiet enough to allow them to do so.

Exactly what being a houseman entails does not become clear to you as a medical student. No one hides the facts, but the awe in which you hold even the most junior of doctors prevents you from taking a critical look at their work. You only hear the edited highlights – the interesting cases and life-or-death dramas – and wrongly assume that the rest of the job goes along in much the same vein. Reality comes as a rude shock, and housemen are frequently dismayed by the amount of non-medical work they have to do.

'I thought being a doctor was about saving lives'

DR GRAHAM HUNT: I thought being a doctor was going to be stimulating and about saving people's lives, but it isn't. I have to do all the bloods and urine samples [that meant collecting them from patients, not producing them himself!], file the results, look for patients' notes and collect notes from the Records Department. I spend the whole day doing rubbish.

'A glorified clerk'

DR ROBBIE KENDALL, A JUNIOR DOCTOR AT A CHILDREN'S HOSPITAL IN SCOTLAND: I'm not enjoying this six months – the trivia side of it spoils the job. When I'm on call, for example, I spend up to an hour giving IV drugs, and another hour or more sticking blood samples into bags, writing forms, and filing pieces of paper. I spend a substantial amount of time doing things that I don't think are medical jobs. They're clerical jobs or nursing jobs. I want to spend time seeing patients, treating patients and thinking about patients, rather than being a glorified clerk.

As it now takes five to six years, and costs more than £50,000, to train a doctor, it hardly seems the most sensible use of time and money for housemen to spend so much of their day on tasks that could be carried out by technicians and clerical staff. Although some hospitals do employ phlebotomists to take blood specimens, and have ward clerks to deal with day-to-day administrative matters, the attitude of others seems to be 'Why pay three people when you can get one mug to do the lot?' It's certainly an effective cost-cutting measure, but one that means housemen spend little time with patients.

Even if every doctor only had to deal with these extra tasks for a year (and many of them do, in fact, have much the same kind of additional duties loaded on to them for several years at SHO – Senior House Officer – level), I would still argue that in those first twelve months they are more impressionable than at any other time in their career, and it is then that they adopt habits which can last a medical lifetime. If housemen are forced to let technical and clerical tasks take priority over contact with patients, this minimises their personal involvement with the people in their care. As I mentioned earlier, the scientific bias of current medical training encourages this kind of impersonal approach and, to counter it, newly-qualified doctors need to spend more, not less, time with patients.

Unfortunately, the longest encounter between a hospital in-patient and houseman often becomes a fact-finding mission for the doctor, and an interrogation for the patient. The process is known as 'clerking' and it follows a standard format drilled into the doctor at medical school: he takes a 'history', gathering information about the patient's past and present illnesses, family, social circumstances, and current medication, then follows this

27

with a physical examination. If you've ever been a hospital in-patient you'll recognise the scene in which the houseman fires questions at you with the force and rapidity of a sub-machine gun:

'Just a few questions, Mr Jones'

HOUSEMAN: Hello there. You must be Mr Jones.

PATIENT: Yes, that's right.

HOUSEMAN: Good, good. Well, just a few questions, Mr Jones. How long have you had the pain?

PATIENT: Well, it started just before my daughter's wedding and that was—

HOUSEMAN: I'm afraid I haven't much time, Mr Jones. Could we stick to the point? Days? Weeks? Months?

PATIENT: Oh. Um. About three months I suppose . . .

HOUSEMAN: Any vomiting?

PATIENT: Well, only very—

HOUSEMAN: No vomiting. Good. Losing weight?

PATIENT: No, I think I'm about the s—

HOUSEMAN: Weight stable. Fine. Bowels?

PATIENT: Well, I do get a bit constipated somet—

HOUSEMAN: Bowels normal. Good. Now if I can just examine your tummy quickly . . . Mmm. Fine. Well I'm sure we'll have you back to work in no time after Mr Slattery's operated on your stomach ulcer.

PATIENT: But I haven't got—

HOUSEMAN: You'll be tucking into four-course meals again before you know it!

PATIENT: But, doctor . . .

HOUSEMAN: What's that, Mr Jones?

PATIENT: I'm having a hernia fixed, not an ulcer . . .

For the houseman, clerking is, at best, a kind of detective game, using clues from the history and examination to help him arrive at a diagnosis. At worst, it is a time-wasting ritual (when, for example, all relevant information is already in the patient's notes), but one which custom dictates he must perform. Dr Kate Pitman, a quiet and rather shy girl, had definitely not enjoyed the endless clerking that was part of her surgical housejob:

'Sundays were horrendous'

Sundays were horrendous because we had up to fifteen patients
coming in to be clerked for Monday's operating list. The most
annoying thing was that nobody would ever read anything you'd
written and I often wondered if I'd put down complete rubbish
whether anyone would have noticed. I used to work every
Sunday for nothing.

Traditional medical teaching stipulates the nature, and order,
of questions to be asked in clerking, and many students find
that once they're familiar with the format, they feel uncomfortable, even irritated, if a patient inadvertently strays from the
path. A standard clerking forces the doctor to play inquisitor
and gives the patient little chance to volunteer anything other
than truncated answers, especially when the doctor is pressed
for time, and sticks rigidly to the traditional line of questioning.
Dorothy Peters, a middle-aged lady anxiously waiting to have
her gall bladder removed, described her experience of being
clerked:

'I didn't get a word in edgeways'

This doctor came to see me and asked me all about the pain –
where it was, how often I got it and the like, and asked about
my family, whether any of them had had gallstones. He didn't
ask about what I ate though, and I thought diet was supposed to
be important with gallstones. I wanted to ask him about that. In
fact, I wanted to ask him about lots of things but he didn't give
me a chance to get a word in edgeways.

With such a sterile protocol in force, it's not surprising that
clerking often leaves the houseman bored and the patient frustrated, and radical changes are necessary to improve the situation.

Doctors must learn how to listen as well as how to talk,
and we must become as adept at uncovering feelings as we are
at detecting physical symptoms and signs. Only then will the
houseman see clerking as something more than an obligatory
questionnaire, and will that first contact with a patient create

the kind of atmosphere in which a more personal bond can develop between them.

Housemen may not relish the more mundane aspects of their job, but it is the long working hours, fatigue and stress which really take their toll on newly-qualified doctors.

Although few have children at this stage of their lives, many do have a spouse or partner who may find it difficult, even impossible, to live with the tired, tense and crotchety person the houseman often becomes. Several of the doctors I spoke to were bitter about the detrimental effects that housejobs had had on their private lives.

'It's had a disastrous effect'

DR HELEN BADCOCK: It's had a disastrous effect on my personal life. And it's not just me. Most of my friends from medical school were in long-standing relationships and there's now not a single one of them left. If you're working a one-in-three and so is your partner, but the days on call are different, then you need a great deal of commitment to keep it going. You also have to make an effort to keep in touch with people, it's very easy to not go out, and you suddenly find a month's gone by and you haven't done anything except work.

Dr Graham Hunt, who had been living with his girlfriend for several years before starting his housejobs:

'Everything outside comes to a grinding halt'

In my first six months I had to go into the hospital every day. It didn't give me a lot of free time to spend with anyone else or have any hobbies or pastimes. Basically for a houseman here everything outside comes to a grinding halt. It's very difficult not to take work home. I was going home tired, and hassled, and that tended to come out on my other half. I didn't even know it was happening until it was too late.

Although housemen complain about some aspects of their work, most seem to enjoy it overall. They accept tiredness and stress, albeit begrudgingly, as part of the job, and in the end, the satisfaction derived from gaining new skills and coping with a demanding and responsible position outweighs the stressful and less enjoyable elements of the work. But how do they feel about the financial rewards for newly qualified doctors? Virtually all the housemen I spoke to had the same, rather mixed, attitude to their pay:

'I work 100 hours a week'

DR HELEN BADCOCK: I think the basic salary's fine. The basic's about £10,200, so with the extra hours on top it's about £16,000 gross [1989 figures]. What I take home each month seems like a lot of money because it's very much more than I ever had as a student, and it's more than most people take home in their first job. But I work, on average, 100 hours a week, yet I earn about the same as some people working 40 hours a week. And we get no perks. So if you think about it cold-bloodedly we are underpaid. We don't get paid enough overtime for working weekends and all night. But on the other hand if you compare our basic salary to nurses and teachers then we're well off.

DR GRAHAM HUNT: When I'm on call my rate of pay is £1.49 per hour. That's lower than the porter's *basic* pay. In fact, it's the lowest rate of pay throughout the hospital.

'We get less money for our overtime'

DR LISA WESTBURY, A HOUSEMAN IN THE NORTH-EAST MIDLANDS: The fact that we get less money for our overtime than we do for the core hours of the week is disgusting, but you can't do anything about it because doctors aren't supposed to complain. In a way it's our fault really because junior doctors just accept the status quo. But we're tied by the need for a reference. If we made a fuss we'd be marked out as troublemakers and we wouldn't get references from our consultants.

The fear of retribution has been a powerful force restraining junior doctors from demanding better hours and rates of pay. Sadly, they have every right to worry about a possible backlash against them, for most consultants want a quiet life and view with disfavour any junior who rocks the boat. References and patronage are vital to get on in medicine, so junior doctors have little choice but to suffer in silence if they are to secure the help they need from the heavyweights of the medical hierarchy.

The hospital career structure which shapes this hierarchy is something that most people know little about, yet it is crucial to understand how doctors progress through the ranks in order to make sense of the roles they play with regard to medical colleagues and patients. In their first year of work, newly qualified doctors are meant to gain basic skills in caring for patients with medical and surgical problems. If, at the end of the twelve months, they are judged to be up to standard, they will become fully registered with the General Medical Council and will be eligible for promotion to senior house officer (SHO) grade.

Many doctors aren't ready at this stage of their career to commit themselves to one particular specialty, so they will continue to gain 'general' experience, working in a Casualty department or on medical or surgical firms which could be considered useful whichever specialty they eventually plump for. Those that have decided on their final career path will opt for SHO jobs in their chosen field – anaesthetics, psychiatry or paediatrics, for example. Since these jobs are of a more specialised nature, they are not deemed suitable for pre-registration training; that means that although the doctor is now afforded SHO status there will be no housemen 'beneath' him on the ward. He'll therefore be expected to perform the duties of a houseman whilst also bearing the responsibilities of an SHO. And he'll still be at the bottom of the firm hierarchy.

There is no set time that a doctor must serve at SHO level before being able to move up another rung of the ladder to registrar grade. Bright young things may enjoy a meteoric rise through the junior ranks if they perform well (in the eyes of their seniors, that is), and pass the necessary post-graduate exams. Others may plod along more slowly, taking several attempts to get the extra qualifications under their belt, and never managing to clinch the prestigious jobs (and influential connections that go with them) which help to guarantee a secure future within their chosen specialty.

Studying for post-graduate exams puts an added strain on

doctors who are already overworked and tired. I remember the months leading up to these exams as being the most miserable of my life. The days and weeks consisted of nothing but working by day and studying by night, made all the more depressing by the knowledge that failure rates in the exams were very high. The elation I felt when I was awarded the letters MRCP (Member of the Royal College of Physicians) after my name had far less to do with pride at joining such an august body of doctors, than with overwhelming relief that I wouldn't have to study for the exam again!

A doctor who makes it to registrar level will probably spend between two and four years gaining further experience in his field, and will be encouraged to undertake a research project of some kind. Original research has become almost mandatory for senior hospital jobs, and many doctors feel obliged to spend a year or more away from the wards, working as a research fellow, in order to gain an MD or, at the very least, to gather material which can be published in medical or scientific journals. 'Publish or perish' is a much-quoted maxim and the advice is more pertinent now than ever before.

The difficulty in securing a senior hospital post is due to the system's pyramid-shaped career structure. There are many more jobs available at junior level than at senior registrar grade, and even fewer posts for consultants. It's therefore inevitable that at every promotion point some doctors will manage to climb to the next rung of the ladder while others fall by the wayside. Very few will give up medicine altogether; anyone who has survived five years at medical school and the hard times as a junior hospital doctor will be reluctant to throw in the towel, especially since they have no training or experience in any other kind of work. Instead, most of those who are forced to give up their first choice of career path will switch to a specialty in which the competition seems a little less tough – doctors still aren't falling over each other to do venereology, so that's always a good bet!

The change to a different specialty may involve a decision to leave hospitals altogether, and head for a career in general practice. In the past, when GPs were held in contempt by a large proportion of the medical profession, a doctor deciding to move into general practice would probably have been chided by his colleagues for casting himself out into a medical wilderness. Times have changed, and with them the status of general practice. Now a doctor will find it difficult to move grudgingly into a career as a GP if he fails to make the grade in some hospital specialty: to satisfy new standards for general practice training a doctor must do at least two years of post-registration hospital jobs in a range of specified fields, and anyone who headed into a specialty early in their career is unlikely to have achieved the requisite breadth of experience. If they can find suitable jobs in the stipulated specialties and stomach the pay and long hours of an SHO for an extra year or more, they may still qualify for general practice, but the battle for those vital training posts is becoming more and more fierce.

Doctors who decide to go into general practice early on in their career may choose to join a 'vocational training scheme' which guarantees them four posts, each for a period of six months, in a selection of different specialties, as well as a year working as a 'trainee' GP. This experience, together with their year as a houseman, will satisfy the training requirements and also provides them with job security for three years – a luxury which few other junior hospital doctors enjoy. Not surprisingly, the places on these training schemes are hotly contested. The stiff competition, together with the prospect of two more years at SHO level, makes the schemes less attractive to doctors who have already spent several years in the junior grades only to abandon their original designs upon a hospital career. As an alternative, they may be able to widen their experience enough to fulfil the requirements for general practice training by doing a couple of six-month jobs in relevant specialties, and by so doing will minimise the time it takes them to become a fully fledged GP.

For those doctors who go on to reach senior registrar level, it may still be a case of 'so near and yet so far' in their bid to secure a consultant post and thereby reach the top of the hospital career ladder. Most doctors expect to spend three to five years as a senior registrar before being accepted for a consultant post, but if they fail to win such a job they may find themselves out of work altogether. Because senior registrars, like all junior doctors, are regarded as being in training posts, they are expected to have gained adequate experience, and therefore to have no further need of training, within a set number of years, usually five. When that period has elapsed they are said to be 'time expired' and they may be forced to leave their post so that another doctor can begin his senior registrar training.

Although efforts are being made to increase the number of consultant jobs throughout the country, there are still far too few to guarantee employment to all the senior registrars in post. For those who become time expired without landing themselves a consultant job the future can look bleak. When their contract with the NHS is terminated their options are few: they must either find alternative funding for a hospital post from sources such as drug companies or medical research bodies, content themselves with short-term locum jobs (taking the place of senior registrars or consultants who are on sick leave, holiday or temporary secondment to another hospital), or look for work in private hospitals either at home or abroad. The scenario of a time-expired senior registrar spending six months of each year working in Saudi Arabia to earn enough money to pay the mortgage and spend the rest of the year with his wife and children back in England is by no means unheard of. Not surprisingly, many doctors are bitter that they must face this kind of uncertain future if they opt for a hospital career within the NHS.

For some doctors there is, of course, a happy ending to their career story. A certain percentage do make it through the ranks and finally win themselves a consultant post. It's possible they'll have spent a good deal of their medical career moving from hospital to hospital around the British Isles, either to gain experience (and good references) from the best departments dealing in their chosen specialty, or simply because they've had to go wherever jobs became available. The situation is often little different at consultant level: few doctors can afford to be choosy and hardly anyone turns down a consultant job, for fear they'll never be offered another one. It's tough luck if your heart and roots lie in Cornwall but you're offered a consultant post in East Grinstead, because once you've accepted the job there's every probability that you'll be there for life. Most doctors seem to make the best of whatever comes their way, with any blighted hopes tempered by the sheer relief of having secured a consultant post at all.

Such is the long and treacherous road which lies ahead of a houseman hellbent on a hospital career. I sometimes think only martyrs and masochists could deliberately choose such a difficult path; if so, then the world of medicine is brimming with both. In reality, most housemen have little idea of the problems ahead of them; they have no time to ponder on the future, for they are much too busy trying to cope with the job in hand.

Almost every houseman I spoke to resented the long hours imposed on them, but it was obvious that they also felt guilty if they moaned about their lot. Their ambivalence stems from a belief that a dedicated doctor brushes aside selfish concerns – a notion induced by the romanticised image of doctors which generously, but mistakenly, portrays us as a selfless and saintly breed. The pressure to be perfect impels housemen to soldier on in silence, but, being human, some feel angry about their hours and rate of pay. Their dilemma exposes a trap that anyone in the medical profession can easily fall into: trying to deny their own human weaknesses, and instead live out the fantasy role of a virtuous and infallible doctor. As long as the myth is perpetuated it threatens to strangle both doctors and patients, with the first hint of its pressure squeezing unsuspecting housemen, like some powerful grip tightening slowly round their necks.

CHAPTER 3

THE CONSULTANT

MOST HOSPITAL PATIENTS await their consultant's ward round with a mixture of curiosity and apprehension. Propped up against their pillows, they are alerted to his arrival by a growing cluster of medical students and junior doctors loitering at the entrance to the ward. Those who have never witnessed 'the boss's ward round' before often expect an imposing figure in half-moon specs and an impeccable suit to stride on to the ward with his train of white-coated acolytes in procession behind him. Some people will see just that, for the old-style consultant who descends from on high and thunders through the ward shouting at staff and patients alike is not yet extinct, though it has to be said that he is one of a dying breed. Other patients will be surprised by their consultant's mild-mannered ways and youthful appearance; the entourage will still be with him, but sauntering along at his side in a relaxed manner.

Whatever type of consultant you meet, you can be sure of one thing: he has worked hard to rise through the ranks and secure himself a place at the top of the medical tree. The competition along the way is stiff, as every doctor who follows a hospital career dreams of winning a consultant post. They hope that at the end of the rainbow this crock of gold lies in wait for them, but the well-worn tracks don't lead everyone to treasure, for there aren't enough spoils to go round. The pyramidal career structure of hospital medicine causes inevitable bottlenecks, with registrars and senior registrars most affected by the jam. Many caught in the crush get trampled underfoot, as others clamber over them, desperate in their bid for the ultimate prize.

Women doctors find it particularly difficult to win their way through to consultant level – a sad fact of life for those patients who would prefer to see a female specialist. In 1986, there were some 14,500 consultants in England and Wales, of whom less than 2,000 were women. At SHO level, the ratio of male to female doctors is approximately 2 to 1, amongst registrars and senior registrars, 3 to 1, and at consultant level the ratio rises sharply to more than 6 to 1. Why this difference as we climb the hospital ladder?

Many women in the junior ranks have no wish to follow a career as a hospital specialist, and so once they have adequate hospital training move into general practice, community medicine and other medical fields. Others would prefer to continue in hospital medicine, but feel unable to pursue such a demanding career and bring up a family as well, so they choose, somewhat reluctantly, to take up alternative medical work. Both groups contribute to the falling proportion of female doctors on the rise through the hospital ranks, but why the further drop at consultant level? Most women who make it to senior registrar grade complete their training and are eligible for a consultant post, so one can only wonder to what degree prejudice accounts for the greater number of male senior registrars being awarded consultant status.

Dr Christine Donaldson, a gentle, motherly woman, married with two teenage sons, worked as a part-time consultant in the north of England. She felt that the biggest problem for women doctors was completing their specialist training while trying to rear a family:

'Women in medicine have a hard time'

I think women in medicine have a hard time but, having said that, women doctors do have it a lot better than many other professions. If you're a woman and single, or married but not intending to have children, then you can compete with the chaps. But if you're married and want a family, then you have a problem. It's very difficult to do your post-graduate training part-time because there is no flexibility within the National Health Service to allow that. If, like me, you're fully accredited and trained before you want to go part-time, then there's a modicum of flexibility within the system, because part-time consultant posts do exist.

Not all female doctors feel, as Dr Donaldson did, that the needs of women in medicine are different from those of men. Although married, Carol Roylance, an outspoken and assertive consultant in obstetrics and gynaecology, had deliberately chosen not to have children during her years of specialist training. She had little sympathy for the idea that women doctors should be given special help to combine a career and family.

'Women expect a little bit more'

I don't think that the fact that women have babies makes them require less training. It might make them require slightly different patterns of training, and I think if you try hard enough and persevere at it, you can get those concessions. The trouble is that most women accept that they're going to follow their husbands around, so they chop and change where they're working, and of course if you don't establish yourself in a place then no one's going to provide you with the facilities that you need when you need them. But that would be the same for a man who followed his wife around. Women seem to expect a little bit more and I'm not sure they're right to do so, really.

Most doctors spend 12 to 14 years in hospital training grades before winning themselves consultant status. Their leap on to the top rung of the hospital ladder guarantees them an enviable degree of authority and kudos and, barring accidents or serious professional misconduct, secure employment for the rest of their career. At consultant level doctors are no longer beholden to some other boss, but such heady freedom is not without its price: they must bear the responsibility not only for their own decisions and actions, but also for those of their junior staff. If gaffes are made, consultants know only too well that the buck stops firmly with them.

One consultant's work may vary enormously from another's, partly as a result of different interests and expertise, but also due to the nature of individual appointments. Teaching hospital responsibilities differ from those in a 'district general' or a specialist referral centre, and research commitments and university links further add to the diversity of consultant concerns. Additional tasks accumulate as consultants become more senior: administrative jobs, committee work, lecturing and examining, all jostling with a continuing commitment to patients under their care.

Whether those patients are predominantly NHS or private depends, of course, on the type of hospital in which a consultant works, and on the nature of his contract with the employing body. Not all consultants work full-time for the NHS. Even those who do are allowed to see some private patients as well, provided their earnings from private practice don't exceed ten per cent of their NHS salary. Part-time NHS consultants can choose the number of hours they devote to NHS duties but they forfeit a proportion of the maximum salary in return for the freedom to earn as much as they want to from private practice. The range of contracts available to consultants gives them the freedom to determine their own level of commitment to both systems of medical care.

How strictly consultants adhere to the letter of their contracts is a matter for debate, even amongst themselves. In recent years they have been the subject of more than a little bad press; even Mrs Thatcher appeared to lash out at them when 'senior government sources' attacked their 'restrictive practices and deeply entrenched attitudes'.[1] Almost all the consultants I spoke to considered such criticism unfair to themselves and most of their colleagues. Many felt that the consultant typically portrayed by the media – insensitive and arrogant, neglecting NHS work in favour of profitable private practice – might bear some resemblance to a proportion of London teaching hospital consultants, but was a gross misrepresentation of the rest of their peers. They grumbled about the media tarring them all with the same brush, and were eager to set the record straight.

So how do NHS consultants spend their working hours? Their responsibilities fall into three broad categories: clinical, administrative and academic, with the balance between these areas varying from post to post. The clinical work brings the consultant in direct contact with patients, and although he

1. © *Sunday Times*, December 13th 1987.

bears ultimate responsibility for everyone under his care, patients on the ward will be managed predominantly by junior doctors, while the consultant takes charge of out-patient clinics. His task there is to see patients referred by GPs or other medical colleagues, to initiate investigations and treatment where necessary, evaluate the results, and, for some patients, undertake long-term follow-up. Assessing a new patient can be time-consuming: the process of conducting a full history and physical examination, explaining conclusions to the patient and outlining any necessary investigations cannot be crammed into a ten-minute slot. As a result, 'new' patients are allotted longer appointments than 'old' ones, and many consultants prefer to see the two groups in separate clinics, dealing with perhaps four or five times as many 'follow-ups' as new patients in any one session.

The workload in out-patient clinics makes it impossible for the consultant to run these alone. He depends very much on help from his junior staff, especially SHOs, registrars and senior registrars, and they, in turn, depend on clinic experience to learn the management of a wide variety of medical problems. Although the consultant may assess a patient on their first visit, when they return for follow-up it's likely they will be seen by one of the juniors on his firm. This lack of personal continuity is a disappointment to many patients, but it seems unavoidable if the consultant is to handle all the new referrals.

Patients who need long-term out-patient follow-up fare worst of all, because they are often exposed to a different doctor on every clinic visit. The nature of current medical training requires junior doctors to change jobs, and often move hospitals, every six or twelve months, and this rapid turnover of staff results in patients seeing a string of unfamiliar faces when they attend for follow-up visits. The consultant's is the one name they recognise, but because of the way labour is divided in the clinic, he is the one person they are unlikely to see.

Patients on the wards don't see much of the consultant either. Although his name dangles on a card above their bed-head, or is scribbled on the charts which hang idly by their feet, they'll probably meet him only briefly during their stay in hospital. Some patients, like Fred Douglas, who had been in hospital for a week following a heart attack, find this disappointing:

'I saw a number of different doctors'

I saw a number of different doctors at first and was never quite sure who was who. One of them was older than the rest and going bald so I assumed he must be the boss, but when they all arrived together one day for a big ward round I realised that the guy in the pin-stripe suit must be the consultant. He was nice enough to me – said 'Hello' and all that – but since he seems to be the one in charge I'd like to have had a longer talk with him and seen him more than the once.

The routine care of ward patients is the province of the junior doctors, with the consultant overseeing their work, and helping with the more difficult or puzzling problems. Hence his fleeting visits on ward rounds, designed to monitor the juniors' medical management rather than promote any close relationship with the patients. Most consultants feel they have enough on their plate without trying to become personally involved with every person on the ward, so although they take responsibility for the patients' care and are informed of their progress, in most cases this watchful eye is maintained from a distance.

All the consultants I met emphasised the difference between their role and that of their juniors. Most felt that the pressure on them to use their specialist skills efficiently gave little room to any notion of a personal relationship with the majority of their patients. In this respect they saw their role as different from that of their juniors (and of GPs for that matter); they saw other doctors as providing the 'ground care' for patients while they functioned in a supervisory capacity, offering in most cases specialist advice, rather than overall, long-term management. Dr Michael Hillier, a 51-year-old consultant in general and renal medicine from North Wales, confirmed this view:

'As a consultant you ought to be just supervising'

I don't think it's possible to look on a consultant as some sort of super junior doctor. I think the roles are often complementary. I mean, what my registrar is doing is really rather different to what I'm doing. I'm not being a super registrar any more than he's being a junior consultant, so I do see a medical firm as being an integrated whole. I provide, well, literally, a consultative role on the wards. Most of the acute general medicine that comes into hospital is pretty bread-and-butter stuff, so as a consultant you ought to be just supervising what's being done, usually very well, by less experienced doctors.

I was talking to a general practitioner recently and he said he rather enjoyed sitting down and talking to the elderly whose main complaint was perhaps one of loneliness. Well, I'd love to be able to do that, believe me. I suppose I'm a bit of a GP *manqué* if you like, but, although this may seem rather like megalomania, it would be a bit of a waste of my skills to do that. I need to go for the jugular, I need to go for the nitty-gritty and maybe leave the social work to somebody else. I've got to satisfy myself that we've got the right diagnosis, and although there may be a lot of social aspects that are important, as long as I recognise they're there I've got to off-load that on to somebody else because that's not really what I'm paid to do.

'I don't take a personal interest in individual patients'

MISS CAROL ROYLANCE: I really think that consultants should consult, and should not be personal doctors for patients. I think that's the best way we can use our resources. I don't think I should be expected to take a personal interest in individual patients, not the way the Health Service is run at the moment. I don't think we can afford it. In the 1980s or even the 1990s in the United Kingdom the only way a person can expect to get personal care and attention is by going privately.

I would hate to think that all NHS patients are doomed to impersonal medical care as Carol Roylance suggests, but I think she is right that, because of the roles consultants are currently expected to fulfil, they are not best placed to provide patients with the individual attention they need and want.

Along with out-patient and ward work, a consultant's clinical responsibilities often include the practice of specialist skills, for the purpose of investigating patients. These procedures do bring consultants in contact with patients, but the setting is rarely conducive to meaningful conversation: pressure of time means that the consultant's aim must be to 'spot the lesion' rather than indulge in a lengthy chat. There are similar problems with many of the therapeutic procedures which consultants carry out: surgeons, for instance, spend longer with their patients than most other doctors, but since the patients are usually unconscious at the time they can hardly use the opportunity for developing personal rapport with the consultant!

The amount of clinical work that a consultant conducts himself is, to some degree, flexible, provided that he has experienced doctors on his firm who can run the show in his absence. How much work he delegates is usually a matter for his own conscience, although in extreme cases, where a consultant is thought to be neglecting his duties, hospital administrators may step in. For some consultants, clinical duties are not intended to form the major part of their work; those who hold appointments with a university, as well as in a hospital, may have responsibility for a relatively small number of patients because their teaching and research commitments preclude greater clinical involvement. Their major interest and ambitions may lie in an academic direction, but most consultants are aware that to maintain credibility with their colleagues they must participate, to some degree, in patient care.

The consultant holding a university post often has responsibility for teaching medical students, and may even be involved in drawing up their curriculum and setting some of the exams they must face along the road to a medical degree. The consultant may well have one or more research fellows employed in his department, and must spend time with them, overseeing, or collaborating on, a variety of research projects. Research generates a great deal more work, especially papers to be prepared for publication and presented at medical meetings. If the consultant is a prestigious figure, or his department publishes research on a 'hot' topic, invitations to lecture and address meetings will probably pepper his diary. Naturally, this means time spent away from the hospital, and while patients may feel aggrieved by the consultant's absence, the profile he maintains, nationally or internationally, may attract funding for research which ultimately benefits some of them. Besides which, trips like these are one of the few perks of the job, so most consultants are determined to make the most of them.

Administration is an aspect of consultants' work which some relish and others loathe. Involvement in administrative matters offers the opportunity for consultants to wield significant power in their hospital or university department. Those who hold posts in teaching hospitals or have strong research interests are most likely to develop a taste for 'empire building' – increasing the facilities, research teams and clinical staff working in their unit, while adding to their own prestige and influence in the process. Their ideas for expansion will go nowhere without strenuous campaigning at an administrative level, so ambitious consultants must devote time and energy to meetings with research bodies, pharmaceutical firms, hospital administrators and others whose support is necessary for their plans to come to fruition.

Even consultants with no designs upon a medical empire may find aspects of administration which they enjoy. For some, committee work provides a new challenge when clinical medicine ceases to stimulate them, so their involvement in administrative matters grows as their clinical interests wane. For other consultants, attending committee meetings is nothing more than a tedious chore, but one which they accept is part of the job. With financial restrictions being forced on many hospitals throughout Britain, every consultant knows he must take some part in administrative matters, even if only to try and protect his 'patch' from the worst of the cutbacks.

Every consultant job is different because the mix of administrative, academic and clinical ingredients is never quite the same. The competition for consultant posts means that applicants can't afford to be too choosy but, nevertheless, most doctors climbing the hospital career ladder do have a preference for a particular type of post (be it an academic one linked to a university, a district general hospital job or one in a teaching hospital), and they work hard to acquire the kind of experience and contacts that will help them to win their job of first choice. Despite this element of self-selection, it seems that different kinds of hospitals don't breed their own consultant clones. I spoke to male and female consultants all over Great Britain and found them to be a disparate crowd; attitudes and ambitions

varied widely, dictated far more, it seemed, by personality than
by geography, medical specialty or the kind of hospital in
which they worked.

Dr Anthony Hall was a consultant in rheumatology and
rehabilitation in a specialist hospital about 100 miles from
London. He courted a mildly eccentric image with his bushy
brown beard perching above a bright bow tie, and his modest
beergut (a legacy of his enthusiasm for real ale) held in check by
the buttons of his navy pin-stripe suit. His academic work meant a
lot to him, for he was ambitious both for his unit and for himself.

'It's essential we're involved in research'

I'm probably not a 'typical' consultant, but I do represent a
distillation of many of the things that consultants have to do. I work
in a centre of excellence which is recognised throughout the
world, but it is an anomalous hospital: a big specialist hospital,
outside London, not associated with a university. Unfortunately,
rheumatology, and perhaps even more rehabilitation, are very
misunderstood subjects, and there's a constant disbelief among
the administrators and among certain colleagues that what we're
doing down here is worth a light. So I have to put a lot of
energy into defending this hospital against all-comers which I
find very irritating.

I don't do a lot of research myself now – I do the odd drug trial
in the clinic and that sort of thing – but mostly I'm directing it
rather than doing it. I don't think a place like this could justify its
existence unless it was prepared to take every opportunity it could
of exploiting the clinical material and expertise available to it. So
it's essential to us that we're involved in research and in education
as well as clinical excellence. There are only two directions a unit
like this can go – up or down – and we're determined to go up.

'The clinical workload is often boring'

MISS CAROL ROYLANCE: The clinical workload is often fairly boring
and routine, so I enjoy the teaching and the research more than
anything else. I would never have taken a job where I was not
able to pursue my research interest. Having a research fellow is
terribly important because as a consultant I can't do the research
myself, but I am able to do it through someone else and that's

absolutely terrific. Because of the research I get to international, national and local meetings and keep up-to-date with the innovative work that's going on in my field and I'm able to present new data on an even footing with people who are pursuing academic careers. I enjoy my research a lot.

Dr Hall and Miss Roylance certainly enjoyed the academic side of their job and the kudos associated with it, but other consultants I spoke to seemed rather weighed down by the work generated by academic commitments. Dr Bob Ayers, a paediatrician in Scotland who held both hospital and university appointments, mused on his own academic involvement:

'I could make life easier for myself'

Right now I have an MD thesis to mark and about forty publications to work on – articles, chapters of books and so on. I could make life much easier for myself if I said, 'Right, we'll cut out all research. We won't make advances, we'll just plod on,' and a lot of people do that, but I do feel that it's part of my job. I think if we observe something unusual then it's worth sharing. It's not all altruistic though – we have to produce research and papers in order to get good junior staff who will come as research fellows and also help with the patient care. I'm aware there's a selfish element to it – I don't want to be left exposed by having bad people working for me – but good juniors benefit the patients and the unit too. If we couldn't get good staff to work here we'd all be in trouble.

For some consultants, particularly those in posts not allied to a university, their departments have neither the staff nor the facilities to engage in research. For others, lack of volition is the major reason for opting out of academic work. Dr Russell Hitchcock, a friendly, open man in his fifties, working in the Midlands as a consultant in general and chest medicine:

'I wasn't enthusiastic any more'

When I first became a consultant I did feel it terribly necessary that I should go on doing research, and for about nine years I always had a PhD or MD student working for me, mainly on cystic fibrosis. I felt it was very important that I go on producing papers – the same drive you have as a senior registrar when you know you've got to produce papers – and that lingered for a bit. Then I found I didn't get anything like the satisfaction I used to get out of it. I suddenly realised that I wasn't enthusiastic any more about trying to push back the frontiers of science.

Dr Hall, the ambitious rheumatologist, was well aware that to achieve success for himself and his unit he needed to wield power at an administrative level. He was also, therefore, a very busy 'committee man'; a political animal whose politics shaped his image of the medical profession.

‘We are elitist as a group’

I'm one of those people who's always being invited on to committees. I do actually enjoy committee work and I'm reasonably good at it. I know how to manipulate and I know how to get the most out of them. It's clear that if we're going to hold our end up against the administration in the Health Service, doctors have got to get involved even more than they have done in the past in looking at management, particularly in a health district like this where the district manager is frankly anti-doctor. He's a Marxist and he doesn't really believe in elitism. And of course, whatever else we doctors are, we are elitist as a group, and unashamedly so.

Mr Geoff Fox, an obstetrician and gynaecologist in North Wales, recognised that his own enthusiasm for administrative matters had grown as clinical work lost some of its excitement:

‘I'm looking for a challenge’

I enjoy the administrative and committee work, and I now spend at least one whole day a week dealing with it. After eleven years as a consultant I know I can do the clinical work and I'm looking for challenge in new areas. I want to be stretched.

Many other consultants could muster none of this zeal for committee work:

'It's all pretty hopeless'

DR RUSSELL HITCHCOCK: You spend an awful lot of time planning and arguing your case, and then find it's all pretty hopeless anyway because there's no money available. I do find that incredibly boring and irritating.

'There's a big danger with the new management'

MR CHARLES MILLINGTON, A PAEDIATRIC SURGEON IN SCOTLAND: I can't be bothered with a lot of the committee work, but you have to do a certain amount of it and there's no point in leaving it. I think consultants should be involved because there's a big danger with the new management structure that the medical opinion is going to be pushed to the side. The managers are going to manage and they're going to make all the decisions.

However much consultants become involved in academic and administrative affairs, they also remain responsible for the clinical care of their patients. Unlike most consultants who concentrate their efforts into one, or perhaps two, of these areas, Dr Hall channelled his apparently inexhaustible energy into all three. His enthusiasm for clinical work seemed to rival that for research and committee matters and he was clearly well satisfied with his own clinical skills:

'Simple things are rather satisfying'

One of the advantages of my line of work is that I see the most desperate cases, like motor neurone disease, at one end, and the simplest things, like tennis elbow, at the other. Because of that, the simple things which other people might find rather irritating are actually rather satisfying to me, because they're the ones that get better and they act as a counterbalance to the incurable patients I look after. I still get immense satisfaction from injecting someone's shoulder joint and curing their capsulitis, because I'm rather good at it. I can fling a needle about much better than practically anyone else I know.

I was curious to know how a man who believed in the elitism of the medical profession handled his patients, and how they behaved towards him.

'I am the big white chief'

GR: Do you think your patients are in awe of you?
DR HALL: Oh I'm sure they are! Well, some of them . . .
GR: Do you think that's useful?
DR HALL: Yes I do. I'm sure. For some patients it's therapeutic
– the fact that I am the big white chief and that I am slightly
eccentric, that I have a beard and a bow tie and go round the
wards in a white coat or pin-stripe suit. There are other patients
to whom that's totally inappropriate, and they are the people one
has to handle in a different way – as friends, or occasionally as
adversaries. The latter are few and far between, but there are
people who have to be handled like that.

Mr Richard Douglas, a 41-year-old consultant surgeon, was a
very different character from the purposeful, ambitious Dr Hall,
but he, too, felt that there were advantages in deliberately
cultivating an image as a consultant which marked him out
from his juniors.

'I never wear a white coat'

I do a ward round before an operating list, just to see the patients
and tell them what I'm going to do, and make sure they
understand what's going to happen to them. I think they take
that better from me, as the man in the suit, rather than yet another
white-coated junior. It's a role-playing exercise really, doing ward
rounds. That's why I never wear a white coat on the wards. It
makes me different from the rest of the team and I think the
patients appreciate that.

I suppose some patients are in awe of me, but I do my best to
make sure they're not. I don't have an ego problem. I don't walk
round like James Robertson Justice. I'm more of a sort to sit on
the edge of the bed, eyeball to eyeball, and hold their hand, to
make them feel they're the most important person in the world at
that time, which is what I think the patients want. It's a public
relations exercise really, and an attempt to give them confidence.

Many consultants echoed this viewpoint, seeing themselves
as a reassuring figure for patients, often more distanced from
them than their juniors (particularly in the case of hospital in-

patients), but believing that this detachment was useful, even vital, to the way they work.

'We need to maintain a detachment'

DR MICHAEL HILLIER: I think we are detached from the patients to a greater extent than the juniors because, by the very nature of our work, we're flitting from one thing to another and I think we need, to some extent, to maintain a detachment to be more objective. I think if you become your patient's social worker and health physician all rolled into one you lose your objectivity and you're not doing the job which you were appointed to do, which is to make sure that the patient gets the best treatment. You can't really manage the firm if you're working on the shop floor; you have to oversee the team and if you try and fulfil *all* the roles I think you'll finish up failing dismally.

The need to oversee the medical care provided by more junior doctors certainly encourages consultants to maintain a watchful eye, often from a distance, rather than become personally involved with every one of their patients. Sheer numbers alone would make that impossible, as Dr Peter Graham, a cardiologist at a modern district general hospital in Wales, pointed out:

'I can't remember the names'

I honestly can't remember the patients' names from one ward round to another unless they're old customers. We have over 1,000 patients going through my ward each year, and 500 patients go through the coronary care unit. I see over 700 new patients a year in out-patients, and between 2,500 and 3,000 out-patients come to my clinic each year. If you add all that up, over 5,000 patients a year come through this hospital with my name on their case sheet and I can't possibly get to know 5,000 people.

Some consultants did feel that they had more of a personal relationship with their private patients. On the whole they spent

51

more time with each one than with individual NHS patients, they dealt with them alone rather than sharing their care with a team of junior doctors, and they continued to see some patients for several years, creating the kind of continuity that was often difficult or impossible to achieve with patients receiving NHS care. Patients who have experienced both NHS and private hospital care often remark on the difference, as did this lady in her early sixties:

'We got fed up with the long waits'

My husband and I took out private medical insurance because we were so dissatisfied with the NHS. In a dire emergency we think NHS hospitals are probably very good – except for the terrible lack of privacy – but at one time I had to make a lot of out-patient visits, and my husband was in hospital twice for minor operations, and we got fed up with the long waits, always seeing a different doctor, and the generally miserable atmosphere. I have twice been in hospital as a private patient and, apart from the welcome privacy of one's own room, and so much nicer food, the general attitude was so different. One saw one's own specialist, he had time to answer one's questions, and all the staff from matron to nurses to ward maids looked and talked as if they enjoyed their work.

Some of the consultants I spoke to told me about the difference between their NHS and private work:

'Patients expect far too much'

MR RICHARD DOUGLAS: I'd like to practise medicine in the NHS like I practise at the private hospital up the hill, where I pop in and see my patients every day, probably just for a social chat, and to see how they are. It means they've got me to latch on to, because they know they'll see me every day while they're in hospital. My NHS patients don't see me every day. Maybe they should. I think that would be the best deal for them, but I do think, quite honestly, that patients expect far too much. They can't have that sort of service given the resources we have, and the way that medicine is structured.

'Private care allows people to buy time'

DR PETER GRAHAM: I don't think the patients I see privately get
any better medical care at all, because the standard of investigations and expertise available is just the same in the NHS.
But I see perhaps 300 private patients a year, compared with the
5,000 NHS patients who come under my care, so who gets the
most personal deal? I can allow more time per private patient: I
see two new, and five review, patients in a whole morning at the
private clinic, but in an equivalent NHS clinic there'll be five or
six new patients and anything up to thirty review patients shared
out amongst me and the juniors.

Private care in my specialty allows people to buy time for
discussion of their condition. You could say it's sad that they
have to do that, but that's because of the way the National
Health Service works. It makes the private work more satisfying
for me because I get to know my private patients more.

The other joy about private work is that it's very relaxing for
me, because I know there'll be very few patients, no bleep to
disturb me and no phone calls. I'm not being constantly
interrupted. It's a pleasure to go, whereas the average National
Health Service out-patient clinic is pretty frantic, which makes it
much harder work.

Dr John Robertson, a Midlands gastroenterologist with a busy
private practice in addition to his NHS work, mentioned, with a
wry smile, the less appealing side of private work:

Sometimes the extra time with private patients is an advantage,
but the other side of the coin is that sometimes people feel that
they've bought your time so they're entitled to go on complaining,
on and on and on, about nothing.

Regardless of private practice's more comfortable pace, and the
greater rapport it allows consultants to build with patients, the
primary motivation for taking on private work is money. A
whole-time consultant's annual NHS salary amounts to between
£27,500 and £35,000 [1988 figures], depending on the number
of years he has been in post, and those with part-time contracts
earn proportionately less. Some consultants receive additional

53

NHS income in the form of a 'merit award'[2] which can boost their annual income by anything between £6,260 and £33,720 [1988 figures]. Attitudes to basic pay varied amongst the consultants I spoke to, but few thought they were adequately rewarded for their NHS work. Some experience difficulties in their first few years because without the on-call payments they received as a senior registrar, they find themselves having to accept a drop in pay when they first take up their consultant post. Other stressful factors for new consultants are the burden of ultimate responsibility for patients and the change in their work role. The transition from senior registrar to consultant was felt by many to be a huge step, and one which brought with it both rewards and difficulties.

'The buck stops with you'

DR RUSSELL HITCHCOCK: The big change that takes place when you become a consultant is that the buck stops with you. You assume responsibility for those people who come in under your care and therefore you've got to get used very much more to making decisions. Yes, there are difficulties but it's certainly much more enjoyable being able to do that. It's what you've trained for and what you've looked forward to doing, so you do it with a sort of glee.

'I could never switch off'

MR RICHARD DOUGLAS: At the start I found it quite a heavy burden. I could never really switch off because here I was, with no off-duty, having to be around and available all the time for every patient who had my name tacked on the end of their bed. And you do worry about them. And lose sleep over some. The trouble is there's no way to get rid of the pressures; you just have to try and switch off from them when you leave the hospital. If you don't, you'll end up cracking up.

So much for consultants' early experiences, but how do they

2. Such awards are supposedly given to consultants for 'distinction and meritorious work in the NHS', although some doctors I spoke to thought they were little more than a seniority payment, rewarding length, rather than quality, of service.

fare after several more years in the job? Dynamic characters, like Dr Hall, thrive on a pressurised and varied work schedule, but other consultants, particularly those in less prestigious hospitals and without an academic appointment, seem more prone to disillusionment.

Mr Richard Douglas, for example, held a post as a surgeon in a district general hospital which involved him in neither academic work nor medical politics, and while he recoiled from the pressures of a more high-powered position, he also recognised the potential for boredom in a 'run-of-the-mill' consultant job.

'Routine dullness can be too much'

Boredom can be a big problem. The routine dullness of a lot of medicine can be too much to take if you're really bright. There are days when I sit down in out-patients and I think 'God, I'll be doing this for the next thirty years, exactly the same.' I don't think there are any easy solutions because the work's always there and it has to be done.

Mr Douglas not only acknowledged that boredom could be a problem, but he was also aware of the effect it might have on his relationships with patients.

'I have to role play'

After you've been in the job a few years, 95 per cent of it is done on automatic drive. It's easy to let any boredom spill over into the way you deal with people. I try my best not to let that happen, but I have to role-play. I put on the grease paint and go to out-patients. I probably push them through quicker now than I used to, but I don't think they necessarily suffer because of that. I cut down to the essentials – I mean, if I see a fellow with a hernia, what is there to say? 'Hello Mr So-and-so. Dr Bloggs says you've got a hernia. Let's have a look at it. Woer, yes, you've got a nice one there. Are you on any pills or tablets? No? Right. Out!' And he's out in a minute. He's hardly got his trousers off when he's pulling them on again. There's no point in me spending any more time with him than that. And I suppose that's not just because I haven't got the time. It's because I can't face mouthing the same old platitudes any longer.

Dr Peter Graham, the cardiologist, had, like Mr Douglas, been a consultant for only six years. It was long enough for him to have become openly disenchanted.

'The pressure seems to be getting worse'

I'm 41 next birthday and I was 34 when I was appointed – young, idealistic, enthusiastic, with lots of ideas. I've still got lots of ideas, but I must admit I do feel a little bit worn down, worn out. I can't really be bothered to read medical literature at night and at weekends, partly because I've got young children so there are more exciting things to do. I'm working bloody hard for the National Health Service and the thought of doing it for the next twenty years leaves me feeling horrible.

It's a very stressful job because we're making important decisions all the time, and the pressure seems to be getting worse. They, the horrible 'they', the administrators, want me to process more sausages on the production line. 'Can't you squeeze a few more into your clinic? Your waiting list's three months long . . .' and it is. My waiting list for a new patient, unless it's very urgent, is three months because I've got so many people being referred to me.

I've got no criticism of the hospital – there's a lovely bunch of consultants working here and the atmosphere's very friendly. I just wonder whether I can continue providing a 'super' service as opposed to a very low-key service for another twenty-odd years. The sparkle has gone and I think, to a certain extent, it's because of the pressure of work.

Not all consultants feel jaded or bored once the initial excitement of the job has dwindled. Those I met who spoke about their work with relish seemed to have retained an eager enthusiasm for the subject of medicine. Dr Michael Hillier said 'There's always something new around the corner which is intellectually stimulating. There are still some fascinating discoveries coming through, and as long as there are new developments and even new diseases it makes life interesting.' Dr Russell Hitchcock was equally confident about the enduring appeal of his job when he said 'The nice thing about medicine is that you are always, always, always seeing things you've never seen before. Certainly a week doesn't go by without you learning something, or seeing some new variation of a condition you've seen before. That's the fascination of medicine.' It was no mere coincidence that both of these doctors mentioned diseases rather than people as the major stimulus to their continuing interest in medical work; many consultants I spoke to expressed similar views.

Of the consultants who were less than satisfied with their jobs, some appeared to be victims of their own drive and ambition, the very qualities which had enabled them to rise to the top of the hospital hierarchy and join the *crème de la crème* of the medical profession. Doctors who triumph in the competitive world of hospital medicine are used to striving and succeeding, and once their consultant post is secured, some feel the loss of a goal to pursue most keenly.

'What challenges are there left?'

DR PETER GRAHAM: As a consultant everything becomes a little bit routine. Perhaps it's a lack of stimulation. Being a junior doctor is exciting because you've always got goals to aim for. In my case it was getting my membership [of the Royal College of Physicians] as quickly as possible, getting a research job, completing my MD thesis, managing so many publications, twenty or whatever, and then getting a consultant job. So I had all these goals and then when I first came here it was to get the department organised, which I've mostly managed to do within about five years. So perhaps you're seeing me in a 'down' year because I haven't a lot of goals to aim for. I find myself thinking: What challenges are there left?

If consultants are sometimes dissatisfied with their job, so are many patients dissatisfied with the lack of personalised medical attention they receive from the NHS. So what can you do if you're unhappy with the hospital care you receive? If you simply want the opportunity to see and talk with your consultant then ask a nurse or doctor if this can be arranged. If it can't, then at least put your queries to one of the other doctors on his team – a little more time and explanation from them may give you all the information and reassurance you want.

What if you have seen the consultant, but aren't happy with

him? It's certainly possible to ask him to refer you to another specialist, but he's under no obligation to do so. Alternatively you can ask your GP to refer you to a different consultant, either on the NHS or privately. What if you've been recommended to a particular consultant and specifically want to see them? I'd suggest discussing the matter with your GP; he may know of good reasons why that consultant wouldn't be the most appropriate person for you to see, and might advise someone else. On the other hand, if he thinks your choice is a good one I'm sure he'd be happy to refer you. If you've chosen to go privately and your GP has agreed to write the referral letter, you can insist on seeing whoever you like since you're paying, but I would still bear the GP's recommendation in mind. He stands to gain nothing by referring you to one consultant rather than another, so in that sense his advice will be unbiased.

Sadly, there are all too many patients disappointed by their experience of NHS hospital care. People often believe the 'conveyer belt' feel of hospital treatment is a reflection of the consultant's poor, or uncaring, service. Consultants' eminence within the medical profession, and the prestige afforded them as a result, make it difficult for patients to see them devoid of mystique and glamour. Blinkered in this way, people fail to accept that consultants are human, and that all areas of their work, including their attitude to patients, are coloured by factors such as ambition, workload, conflicting responsibilities, boredom, money and stress.

Certainly some consultants are more interested in the diseases, and less in the people, that they treat. This is an attitude which current medical training instils in all doctors, and which we encourage in consultants by looking to them for highly specialised 'expert' knowledge and a commitment to clinical research. In addition, the role that consultants play for patients is heavily influenced by the structure of the medical system in which they work. That structure may change in the future, if the number of junior doctors is reduced and consultants have to become more involved with emergency medical care, but for the moment their role remains distinct from that of their juniors, and is one which, rightly or wrongly, tends to preclude personal relationships with the patients under their care.

All of us – both doctors and patients – need to think hard about the function we want consultants to fulfil. If they are to be the intellectual elite, the scientific specialists, the pioneers of new techniques for investigation and treatment, do we also expect them to be kind, attentive, people-orientated doctors who deliver a personalised medical service when we need hospital care? I think it's impossible for consultants to perform both roles, at least while their training encourages disease, rather than people, to be the focus of their attention, and while their diverse responsibilities and vast numbers of patients make a 'supervisory' service the only one they can realistically provide.

In the current political and economic climate there is no prospect of consultant numbers rising sufficiently to make any significant difference to the volume of patients under their care, but if individual attention and a greater degree of continuity could be provided by doctors in the junior and middle grades, patients might feel happier about the consultant's more remote role in their medical management. Looking to other doctors for 'personalised medicine' is in no way meant to let consultants off the hook; it may, however, prove the most effective way of ensuring well-rounded hospital care which incorporates the best of high-tech medicine with genuine concern for the ailing individual.

CHAPTER 4

THE GENERAL PRACTITIONER

FOR MOST PEOPLE in Britain, their local doctor's surgery is the first port of call when they want medical advice or treatment. The 'average person' consults their general practitioner four to five times per year, and although this means that people tend to have more contact with GPs than with other kinds of doctors, myths and misconceptions about GPs still flourish, just as they do about their hospital colleagues.

What image do you have of your GP? Is he (or she) a grumpy pen-pusher, eager to dispense of you with a prescription rather than listen to your problems? Or perhaps an overworked soul who tries hard but is always too rushed to deal with matters as you'd really like? Or is your GP a saint – courteous, kind, caring and available whenever you need him? I suspect that even if your doctor appears to fit neatly into one of these categories, he is, in reality, a much more complex character, whose 'doctor' image may mask much of the person inside.

To many people a GP is merely the hospital specialist's poor relation, and the profession itself does little to dispel this hackneyed image. Both junior and senior hospital doctors are sometimes shamefully ignorant about the work of general practitioners, and so fail to value their skills and knowledge. As I'm a GP myself, this may just sound like sour grapes and I don't mean to give the impression that GPs are faultless on this score. Some are every bit as entrenched in their attitude towards consultants, but at least all general practitioners can argue that they have, at some time, worked in hospitals, whereas precious few doctors pursuing a hospital career have ever tried being a GP.

The veneration of hospital specialism and the belittlement of general practice began in the late 1800s and has been kept alive in the 20th century by hospital doctors' attitudes and the nature of medical-school teaching. For generations, as burgeoning diagnostic and therapeutic possibilities made the hospital specialties more numerous and more prestigious, vocal and influential specialists perpetuated the notion of GPs as 'second-class' doctors who had 'fallen off the hospital ladder'. They viewed GPs as Jacks of all specialties and masters of none, fit only to treat minor illnesses and expected to refer anything more serious to 'first-class' hospital consultants. Medical students had little reason to question this image, for until recently their three years of hospital-based training were balanced by no more than a week or two's experience in general practice. Although departments of general practice have now been established in many universities, with a modest increase in curriculum time being devoted to the subject as a result, the overwhelming majority of a student's clinical training still takes place in hospitals. In an environment where consultants are not only first in the pecking order, but are teachers and role models as well, it's easy to see why medical students have, for many years, held them in higher esteem than GPs, of whom they learnt little during their training.

The tide of opinion is beginning to turn, however. General practice has become a more popular career choice amongst medical students in recent years, reflecting a change in hospital career prospects. As competition for senior posts in almost all hospital specialties has increased, many newly qualified doctors have been daunted by the lack of job security within the hospital system and so have opted for general practice instead. This might seem to earmark general practice as a 'second choice' field, but there is also a growing number of doctors deciding to become GPs for positive, rather than negative, reasons. This reflects another change, this time in the image of general practice within the profession, which began to improve as some GPs spoke out against the widespread denigration of their medical role. A movement gathered force, intent on raising the standards and morale of general practitioners, and, as a result, the College of General Practitioners (later to become the

Royal College) was established in 1952. The College has done much to improve general practice by pressing for more teaching in the subject at both undergraduate and postgraduate level, by helping to establish a new system of GP training, and by encouraging general practitioners to undertake more research in their own field of work.

Although the standards of general practice are generally superior to those twenty or thirty years ago, there is still considerable variation from doctor to doctor and from practice to practice. Two patients, both living in London, told me about their GPs, highlighting the good and bad ends of the general practice spectrum:

'I've always found everyone very helpful'

I belong to an excellent practice where there are three doctors, two male and one female. I can make appointments with any doctor, and usually don't have to wait long to be seen – always the same day if it's an emergency. I've always found everyone in the practice, including the receptionists, very helpful. An information sheet for patients advises us at what time of day to telephone if we want to speak to a doctor and the few times when I've really needed a home visit I've never had a problem getting one of them to come round.

'My GP's awful'

I think my GP's awful but he's the only one close enough to get to. The surgery itself is pretty depressing, especially the waiting room, with nothing on the walls but a few notices that have been there for years. You can't book an appointment so you either have to queue outside the surgery for ages before it opens, or go down mid-morning when it's already packed, and be prepared to wait for hours. My friend's doctor has a nurse who runs a Well Woman clinic for smears and things but my doctor doesn't have anything like that.

The disparity between practices exists not only because individual GPs responded with varying enthusiasm to calls for change and improvement, but also because GPs can, and do, choose to practise in quite different ways. Some like working alone while others prefer to be part of a group practice; some hold surgeries in modern purpose-built health centres, others in converted houses or even their own homes; some work closely with a range of other health professionals (such as the practice nurse, health visitor, district nurse, midwife, physiotherapist, psychologist or counsellor), while others are less keen on a 'team' approach and so have more sporadic contact with others involved in the care of their patients. Although GPs are of necessity generalists, dealing with problems ranging from the psychiatric to the obstetric, the neurological to the gynaecological, and with every age group, from infants through to the elderly, some have specialist interests which they use and develop by working at a relevant hospital out-patient clinic for one or more half-days each week. Other GPs spend sessions away from their surgery working, for instance, as a factory doctor or school doctor, or attending various medical committees. Factors like these make general practice a very flexible and varied field of medical work, which is why many doctors choose it in preference to a career in hospital medicine.

If you've ever tried vainly to speak to your doctor during the day and have been told repeatedly that he's busy, you may well have wondered 'Busy doing what?' Surely surgeries and home calls can't fill every moment of his day? It's true that consultations and visits don't eat up the entire week but there are numerous other elements to a GP's work which have to be fitted in somewhere. So how do GPs spend their day? Until recently I worked in a health centre in the London suburbs, and although it was an extremely busy practice with lengthy surgeries, my timetable there was probably not unlike that of many other GPs around the country.

The day began around 8.40 a.m. at an informal meeting with my six partners, and sometimes with health visitors or district nurses, to discuss problems or matters of interest that we felt should be shared. Once or twice a week we saw a drug rep at this early meeting, for a quick update on their company's products. My surgery began at nine and usually ended sometime between noon and one p.m., after I'd seen 25 to 30 patients. I might have one or more home visits to do during the lunch hour and about once a week would have a lunchtime meeting to attend. This was also the only time during the day when I could go to the bank, supermarket, post office or shops; domestic needs had to be squeezed in somewhere as I have no wife at home to take care of them for me!

Back at the practice around 2.15 I would dictate hospital referral letters that were needed for any patients seen during the morning surgery, and deal with the day's mail and repeat prescriptions. At 2.30 or 3.00 the afternoon surgery began, ending at about 6 p.m. after I'd seen another 20 to 30 patients. More referral letters went into a dictaphone machine, extra repeat prescriptions were signed and insurance reports written out before I set off for home at around 6.45. Once a week I was on call from 5.30 p.m. through to 8.30 the following morning for any of our practice's 20,000 patients who wanted an urgent visit or telephone advice. In addition, I was on call for a full 24 hours at the weekend once or twice a month.

Some evenings, apart from those spent on call, were also devoted to medicine. Once a month the partners met to discuss either business matters or clinical topics. The latter gave us an opportunity to review, and, if necessary, update our treatment of common conditions like high blood pressure or asthma, and also to discuss ways of improving the day-to-day organisation of the practice. Other useful evening meetings were held at the local teaching hospital; they provided an opportunity to meet hospital colleagues and keep abreast of new methods for investigation and treatment being used in their departments.

Our practice was undoubtedly a very busy one and the demands could become overwhelming at times. We recognised the need for a regular 'breather' and so (as most GPs in this country do) each partner took a half-day off each week, in addition to their annual five weeks' holiday and one week's study leave (for attending academic courses). I also spent some time away from the practice each week, working at home doing medical journalism. Although the practice's workload was heavy, the partners tried to encourage one another's special interests as much as possible, and, as a result, we all found the work very satisfying.

As a patient you may not have realised the multiplicity of tasks your GP undertakes in a day, nor the diversity of his work. Ted Reynolds, a 54-year-old post office worker, thought his GP's job must be repetitive and tedious:

'It must be a depressing job'

I don't go to my doctor very often – once or twice a year at the most. He always seems to be very busy, if the packed waiting room is anything to go by. I think it must be a bit of a depressing job, seeing nothing but sick people, and rather boring at times, especially during the winter when there must be an endless stream of people with coughs and colds and bad chests.

That's certainly not the way I see general practice, and Dr Stephen Kerr, a phlegmatic man of 61 who worked in a large health centre in Oxfordshire, also found his work anything but boring. He mentioned two aspects of the job which he particularly enjoyed:

'The big attraction is the variety'

The big attraction of general practice is the variety. You never know what's going to come through the door next, and you're switching from one train of thought to another ten times an hour. Another big attraction is that, as a GP, you're the first point of contact with the patient, whereas when you're working in hospitals almost everything you see is 'second-hand'.

Dr David Cohen, a single-handed, Jewish GP in London, was unimpassioned about much of general practice but he, too, liked its variety, and enjoyed the freedom of being his own boss:

I think I've got a bit of a grasshopper mind and if I were a surgeon I'd get terribly fed up doing the same operation for three or four hours. I quite like having something different to deal with every few minutes. I suppose you are also, to a fair extent, your own master in general practice and can do things the way you want to. One of the few advantages of being single-handed is that I can have a holiday when I want to. If I want to be off every Christmas, I can be, as long as I'm prepared to pay a locum.

Dr Henry Winterton, a jovial and vivacious 58-year-old GP in the West Country, cited different reasons for his love of general practice:

'I enjoy being of assistance'

If I was rich I would pay to do general practice, I enjoy it that much! I enjoy talking to people. I like the one-to-one contact with patients. And without meaning to sound creepy about it, I enjoy being of assistance to other people. Most of us have in us a slight desire to serve which is very frustrated nowadays. In the old days practically everyone was a servant in some sense; 80 per cent of the population were serving the other 20 per cent which of course wasn't satisfactory, but it did mean you could be of assistance to others.

I also have this great 'hobby' of homeopathy which can turn a boring surgery into a fascinating and exciting adventure, so that's one big 'plus' for me.

Because many GPs live close to their surgery they can often manage to get away from work and relax at home for at least a short while in the middle of the day. As a junior hospital doctor I found it impossible to set foot outside the building during the day because my bleep would invariably go off and summon me back. When I lived in hospital accommodation, as many junior doctors do, this meant that I was incarcerated in the hospital complex from one end of the week to the other, briefly coming into contact with the outside world at weekends. General practice has certainly improved my quality of life in this regard, and the opportunity to relax away from work during the day is something that many GPs appreciate.

One fundamental difference between GPs and hospital doctors is, of course, the context in which they treat patients. As a GP I can offer care to whole families, for many years at a stretch. Hospital doctors tend to treat individuals, and for many patients they provide care for a limited time only – during a specific illness, for example. Delivering medical care in the community, rather than in hospital, helps me to see a patient's illness against the background of their life; I may know a person's parents, spouse, and children, and have made visits to their home, and regularly hear news about their work, holidays, and other domestic events. I see people when they're healthy as well as sick: contraception, travel vaccinations, antenatal care, cervical smears and routine children's immunisations are all examples of services which bring me into contact with people when they are well, reminding me to think of patients not only in the 'sick role' but also as individuals going about their normal daily lives. In this way, general practice provides opportunities for getting to know patients well, and so adds a personal touch to doctoring which I, and many other GPs, find deeply satisfying.

Dr Angela Leigh, a friendly 61-year-old GP in a four-doctor Midlands practice, described how her involvement with patients' lives gave her great pleasure:

'Total involvement with families'

The total involvement with families is what I enjoy most about being a G P. There's a wholeness, a completeness, to helping people with all aspects of their lives. In general practice you're not just treating illnesses, you're looking after people. Preventative care is a side of general practice that is continuing to grow and I find that interesting. Of course, preventative care can be boring if you see it as something that has to be got through, but if you see it as part of the whole aim to improve people's health and as a way of getting more involved with them, then it's very enjoyable.

I run a Well Woman clinic which is less rushed than an ordinary surgery. Because we make the appointments longer you have a chance just to talk with patients, and it's in that 'just talking' that important things come out. In general practice you're often not dealing just with a person's illness but with their whole social circumstances, and their emotional problems, and I enjoy that side of things.

Although many GPs enjoy the human contact involved in their work, patients are sometimes less satisfied with the personal element of their care. The growth of large health centres and the trend for GPs to practise in groups, rather than singly or in pairs, has helped doctors to offer facilities and services which small practices find it difficult to provide. On the other hand, large practices in purpose-built premises can seem impersonal to patients, and many hanker for the trusted and familiar family doctor of bygone years. Marjorie Saunders, a Midlands housewife in her fifties, was far from happy with her five-doctor practice:

'The place doesn't feel friendly'

It's a bit too much like a hospital for me. All very modern and clean, I know, but somehow the place doesn't feel friendly like I remember my old doctor's surgery did. That was part of his own home and his wife acted as receptionist. He had a huge armchair he used to sink back into, and a big brown leather couch which creaked terribly when you got on and off it. It was a small place, not like this new surgery which is too big, with too many receptionists and doctors, to feel welcoming.

Margaret Wilkes, a London pensioner, also had reservations about her large health centre practice:

'I never know who's going to come'

The doctors don't seem to stay long there. I was under one lady doctor, but she was only there for a year, and now I'm under one of the others. When I need them to visit me I never know who's going to come – it could be any of the doctors. With my old G P it was always him I'd see. I was with him for 32 years before he retired so it was like losing a friend when he went.

Some patients are obviously critical of today's GPs and the way they practise but is the modern general practitioner really incapable of delivering the kind of continuous personal care that so many people want? I don't believe so, for efficiency and organisation need not be at odds with compassion and commitment. Unfortunately, there are some GPs who show little interest in their patients as people, and who can justifiably be criticised for the perfunctory and fragmented care they deliver. But even those doctors who want to offer continuity of care sometimes find it difficult to provide. Dr Hilary Taylor, a 34-year-old GP in a busy health centre in the London suburbs, felt that poor continuity of care for patients was not always the doctor's fault:

'*They* have to put a bit of effort in too'

There are six doctors in this practice and a number of patients do complain that they see a different one every time they come. But often the reason that happens is because people ring up and want to be seen immediately. If it's an urgent problem we'll always fit them in the same day, but they have to see whichever doctor has a space free. Quite often it turns out that the problem isn't really urgent, it's just more convenient for them to be seen that day than the next, and it annoys me if those people then moan that they didn't see their usual doctor. If they'd only been prepared to wait another day they could've seen whoever they liked.

Another problem is that some patients seem to deliberately shop around amongst the doctors. That's fine if they're trying to find out which one they get on best with, and will then stick with them, but sometimes they just don't like a doctor's advice, so they move on to another one, and when they don't like what he advises they'll try the next, and so on. I really don't think any of us is so forbidding that patients can't tell us when they're not happy with our treatment, but rather than discuss it with us, some people will just go and see another doctor and try and get what they want out of him. That's a hopeless situation because no one gets to know the person well enough to find out what's really troubling them, and because of that they carry on being dissatisfied. Some people seem to think that anything that's wrong between them and the doctor is automatically the doctor's fault, and I do wish they would realise that *they* have to put a bit of effort into the relationship too.

Perhaps Dr Taylor's comments seem harsh on patients, but the point she makes is an important one to take on board. I'm a firm believer that you get the best out of a doctor when he knows you well, particularly if you have a difficult or long-standing problem. It may seem easier to change GPs than challenge one you're dissatisfied with, but if you stay with the same doctor, air your views and ask for explanations, you probably stand more chance of getting the understanding you want than if you start back at square one with someone new. You work at relationships with family, friends and colleagues, so why not with your doctor too?

Of course if your doctor won't listen, you're on a losing wicket and, sadly, complaints about inattentive, preoccupied GPs are all too common. Marsha Seymour, a 25-year-old West Indian girl, had this to say of her GP:

'He's not listening'

I wish he'd listen more. When I'm telling him what's wrong with me he's often reading through my notes, or writing something, not listening to what I'm saying. It's the same with the kids. He dives in and puts a stethoscope on their chest before I've finished telling him what the problem is.

Language problems may compound the communication difficulties if doctor and patient do not share the same mother tongue. This has become a more common problem as the immigrant population in Great Britain has grown and as the number of overseas doctors working here has increased. One patient I met highlighted the way in which language difficulties may add to a patient's, or parent's, anxiety:

'We found it impossible to understand'

I think that all foreign doctors in this country should take elocution lessons. Last year our baby daughter became very ill and had to go into hospital. We found it impossible to understand the African locum who was working at our GP's surgery, or the Indian doctor at the hospital, because of their accents, and it was very distressing for us. Eventually we specifically asked to see our own GP, who's English, and he explained everything clearly to us.

Language barriers may be hard to overcome unless an interpreter is readily available, but what about problems of communicating with an apparently inattentive doctor? If GPs enjoy working with people (which most of us claim that we do), why are we frequently portrayed as a brusque, disinterested lot, hurriedly scribbling prescriptions instead of listening to our patients? Undoubtedly, there must be some doctors who aren't really interested in their patients' worries, and others who are simply poor at conveying their concern, but for many GPs it is the pressures of the job that sabotage their efforts to lend a sympathetic ear.

For Dr Andrew Smith, a 37-year-old Wiltshire GP, the constant interruptions which occurred during his surgeries made him tense and unable to give patients his full attention:

'I get so wound up'

I think I'm probably the most open and approachable of the partners at my practice so I tend to attract patients with psychosomatic and emotional problems. I don't mind that, but it's difficult to deal with their problems if we keep being interrupted. Sometimes I find myself trying to deal with a patient, answer a phone call from a consultant, and sort out a receptionist's administrative problem all at the same time. I get so wound up I feel like an elastic band about to snap.

Dr Hilary Taylor found that short appointments made communication with patients less than satisfactory:

'We run out of time'

I see about eight patients an hour so that's only about seven minutes per person. Often it isn't nearly enough to deal with the problems they've brought to me, but if we gave everyone longer appointments I would either have to see fewer people in each surgery, or make the surgeries longer, and then there wouldn't be enough time in the day to do visits and paperwork. It's a terrible problem. Often by the time I've dealt with the medical problem we've run out of time so I can't sit and discuss the treatment, or give as much explanation and reassurance as I'd like to. I'm sure some patients don't open up to me as much as they would if the surgery pace was slower and more relaxed. But I can't see any way round the problem.

There are no easy solutions to practical problems like these. Longer appointments might seem sensible, but, as Dr Taylor pointed out, GPs would then see fewer patients each day, possibly causing unacceptable waiting time for consultations.

Doctors would feel less harassed if their surgery time was free of interruptions, but telephone calls are inevitable, both from patients and professional colleagues, any one of whom may need immediate information or advice. More GPs, especially in densely populated areas, would help to reduce each doctor's workload, but with present restrictions in force no such help is in sight. Sadly, the status quo looks set to continue; for the overstretched GP the job will inevitably remain stressful, and patients may be the ones who are shortchanged as a result.

Given that your GP (and his practice staff) may be very pressurised at work, what can you do to make sure you get a good service from them? Firstly, you need to find out as much as you can about the way the practice runs, so that you can use it to your best advantage. Ask if your practice has a leaflet giving details about surgery times, special clinics, out-of-hours cover provided, as well as instructions on how to obtain repeat prescriptions or a home visit. If it doesn't, then get this information from one of the receptionists and keep it somewhere safe, so you can refer to it when necessary.

Think about what you want from your GP and ask in advance how you can go about getting it. Where possible, consider the difficulties the doctor and his staff face and try not to add to them! For instance, if it's telephone advice you're likely to want, find out at what times the doctor is available to talk on the phone. Knowing that, you will avoid disturbing the GP when he's trying to deal with other patients in surgery, and are less likely to get hurried, inadequate advice.

If you're trying to decide whether to ask for a home visit or not, stop and think first about your reasons for doing so. If you would have genuine difficulties getting to the surgery, or think that you (or whoever you're requesting the visit for) are too ill to leave home, then I think most GPs would agree that a home visit is necessary. Be honest about whether the real reason you want a house call is because it's more convenient than going to the surgery, and then ask yourself if that's fair on the GP or the other patients he could see while he's spending time coming out to see you. I can remember one patient who told me she couldn't possibly come to the surgery because she was waiting for the TV repair man to call – not the kind of request that endears a patient to their doctor!

72

Whether to a doctor or receptionist, always try to explain yourself clearly. I know that may be difficult, especially if you find the person intimidating or unsympathetic, but the more information you give about the problem, your reason for being worried, and the type of help you're after, the more likely you are to get a satisfactory response. Naturally, you are entitled to expect the doctor to be communicative and helpful, but if you want to reap benefits for yourself it is important that you try to be communicative and helpful too. Whatever mutual understanding you can foster with your GP and his staff will go a long way to securing a good relationship between you.

A GP must obviously try and meet his patients' needs if his practice is to survive and flourish, but what many patients may not realise is that he must also be an effective businessman. When changes proposed in the Government's 1989 Health Service White Paper are implemented, GPs will have to concentrate even more on the financial and administrative aspects of their work. Unlike a hospital doctor, whose NHS income is determined by Department of Health salary scales, a GP's earnings depend to some extent upon item-of-service fees. Immunisations, cervical smears, contraception and antenatal care are just some of the services for which a GP can, at the time of writing, claim individual payments from the local Family Practitioner Committee. A GP who achieves high infant immunisation rates and a good take-up rate for cervical smears, and assiduously submits claims for all the work he has done, will earn more than one who offers the same services haphazardly and is forgetful about recovering fees. In this way, the system provides dual incentives for a GP to organise his practice efficiently: while benefiting patients by expanding the services available, he can also gain financially himself.

Medical school gives students some idea of how to be a doctor but it doesn't teach them anything about the business side of general practice. Since GP vocational training became mandatory in 1981, most doctors learn the rudiments of practice finance and organisation in their GP trainee year. For those who entered general practice before the late 1970s, there was no such preparation. As few of them had any interest or aptitude for matters of business, the real world of general practice provided something of a rude awakening.

'It's regrettable that GPs have to be businessmen'

DR HENRY WINTERTON: I never really thought about the business side of general practice when I went into it. It's a part of general practice which perhaps we ought to be introduced to a bit more as students. It ought to be emphasised that it is important to have a certain inkling about business matters. But I do think it's most regrettable that GPs have to be businessmen. I think that the sort of qualities that go to make a good businessman are very, very different from the ones that go to make a good doctor, and to be good at both is a very rare thing.

Several doctors I spoke to also complained that they had been the victims of unscrupulous older partners who loaded a great deal of work on to their shoulders and paid them a pittance in return. I heard of several practices in which a senior partner, who handled virtually all the financial matters alone, had embezzled many thousands of pounds from practice funds, while naïve junior partners remained oblivious to the trickery going on under their very noses. Legally binding partnership agreements are now more common, and every doctor in a practice which has such a contract must abide by its rules or face legal action. An increasing number of partnerships also employ a practice manager who supervises administrative work including the financial aspects of practice business. Measures like these mean that GPs are less likely to suffer because of their own lack of business acumen.

Of the young GPs who have been benefiting from greater openness and equality within practices, many are women. The number of women GPs in Britain has nearly doubled in the last ten years – from 3,500 in 1977 to just over 6,000 in 1986 – a change which has increased patient choice and greatly pleased those who prefer to see a female doctor. Many women are attracted to general practice because they feel it's more compatible with family life than a hospital career. On-call duties for a GP can be arduous at times, but are rarely as bad as the one-in-three and one-in-four rotas which many women training for a hospital career have to endure for years as they rise through the junior ranks. It has also been easier, at least until now, for women to get part-time work in general practice than in hospitals. Unfortunately, the Government's new contract for doctors makes part-time partners less attractive to practices, so we may see a fall in their numbers in future years – a tragedy for those women whose training may be wasted, and for the patients who want a female doctor but find none available at their surgery.

Whether female or male, all GPs find out-of-hours cover an extra strain, and I've yet to meet one who enjoys getting out of bed to answer calls during the night. However irksome the work may seem at times, we cannot duck the fact that we are responsible for our patients 24 hours a day, 365 days a year, and have to ensure that medical care is available for them at all times. Deciding exactly *who* should deliver that care outside normal surgery hours presents GPs with a dilemma which isn't easy to resolve.

Privately run companies offer deputising services in some parts of the country to provide medical cover outside normal surgery hours, but GPs are sharply divided about the ethics of using them. The doctors employed by the deputising firms are all fully qualified but will have no personal knowledge of the patients they are called to see. They may be hospital doctors or GPs supplementing their income with some night or weekend work, or doing deputising sessions to earn a living while they try to find a more permanent general practice or hospital post.

Dr Hilary Taylor shared night and weekend duty with her partners and described their reasons for doing the work themselves:

'I'd never feel certain of the care'

I wouldn't want to use a deputising service because I'd never feel certain of the quality of care the patients got out-of-hours. I also think patients prefer to see a familiar face if they need to call a doctor out, so I think it's only right that my partners and I should do our own night work. Lots of problems that people phone you about just need telephone advice and I think it's important for them to learn that they don't always need a doctor to visit. If a deputising service is doing the night work a doctor will always go out, even if the problem is only a cough or cold, and I think that leads people to become complacent. They'll call the deputising service for the slightest thing because they know they won't be refused a visit.

Dr Angela Leigh explained why she had started to use a deputising service for night calls:

'I lost hours sleep'

I've only used a deputising service for the last two years and started to just because I was getting older. There was a time when I could go out on a night call, come back and get straight back to sleep, but then I found I wasn't. I was taking much longer to get off to sleep. So I didn't just lose the sleep of the actual time I was out on the call, I lost two or three more hours' sleep as well. And I was less able to cope the next day. I feel that, as I am now, I'm giving a better service to the patients by using the deputising service from eleven p.m. to seven a.m.

Patients' views on out-of-hours home visits seem to vary considerably. One survey published in 1988[1] found that patients under the age of 60 were happier with a visit from their own GP than from a deputising doctor, but that people over 60 seemed equally satisfied with visits by deputies and GPs. This may simply mean that older people have lower expectations, or are more reluctant to voice criticisms, than younger people, but it's possible that there is a real difference in the service they receive from deputising doctors and GPs. We certainly need more studies to examine the out-of-hours care provided in general practice in order to find out what patients really want and whether it is possible for GPs to meet those demands.

1. Bollam, M., McCarthy, M., Modell, M., 'Patients' assessment of out-of-hours care in general practice', *British Medical Journal*, 1988; vol. 296, pp. 829–32.

Unfortunately, GPs who do their own night and weekend duty usually have no time off afterwards to recover. Most will have a full day of surgeries and visits to face, even if they've been woken several times during the night. The prospect of an evening on call, sandwiched between one hard day's work and the next, can make even the most diligent of GPs grumpy, which explains why your normally charming doctor may growl like a bear with a sore head when you phone him at night!

Although the medical problem may not be a serious one, people often want a visit because they are desperate for reassurance. Unfortunately, the doctor may be equally desperate for sleep. Tempers may then flare if either party senses that the other is putting their own needs first. I'm sure at times patients have resented me when I've insisted that telephone advice is all that's necessary for their child's temperature or cough; they probably thought I was being selfish and uncaring. But I've felt equally resentful of patients demanding a visit in the middle of the night for diarrhoea or period pains. I can't help thinking that they're selfish and uncaring too. The trouble is, both patients and doctors are human, but when either of us is at a low ebb we'd prefer to forget the other's needs and pander only to our own. More imagination and consideration on both sides would go a long way to solving the problem.

Perhaps it seems I'm exaggerating the stresses and strains of general practice but several studies appear to bear out my claims. In 1981 it was estimated that there could be as many as 3,000 practising GPs who are alcoholics,[2] and another study concluded that GPs were nearly three times as likely to become alcohol dependent as other people of the same social class.[3] Along with other doctors, GPs are roughly three times more likely to commit suicide than the general population and twice as likely to be admitted to a psychiatric ward. There can be little doubt that stress associated with work contributes to these disturbing figures.

In the course of my research I spoke to several GPs who had

2. Allibone, A., Oakes, D., Shannon, H. S., 'The health and health care of doctors', *Journal of the Royal College of General Practitioners*, 1981; vol. 31, pp. 728–31.
3. Murray, R. M., 'Alcoholism amongst male doctors in Scotland', *Lancet*, 1976; vol. 2, pp. 729–33.

suffered drug or alcohol addiction. The stress of general practice was frequently mentioned as one of the main factors contributing to their problem. Dr Chris Perryman, a 43-year-old GP, thought some of his difficulty coping with work was due to an underactive thyroid gland which had been undiagnosed and untreated for several years, but the pressures inherent in being a GP were also part of the reason he had become addicted to tranquillisers and alcohol:

'You're supposed to put everything right'

My overriding conviction during my first few years as a GP was that patients' health depended on me, so I couldn't let them down. I told all my patients I was always available and would talk to them whenever they needed me and I guess they took advantage of me. Many of the problems that people brought to me weren't strictly 'medical', more emotional and psychological, and because I had no training in counselling I felt impotent, unable to help. But because you're there, and you're the doctor, you're supposed to put everything right, and that was a huge pressure.

Part of the problem was that I'm from a working-class background and I was trying to prove I was as good as all my middle-class colleagues. It was impossible for me to say that I couldn't cope – and that goes for a lot of doctors. I feel strongly that it should be compulsory for doctors to have regular physical and psychological health checks because we're all so reluctant to ask for help.

I've conquered the addiction to tranquillisers and alcohol now. Part of the reason I feel better able to cope with general practice is that I've realised GPs can't cope with patients' ill health all on their own. Some people need advice about housing, marital problems, things like that, and if you involve other professionals – nurse practitioners, social workers, even teachers and solicitors – this takes a big strain off the doctor. It's crucial to discover you're not on your own, that you can work as part of a team. And patients don't think any the less of you because you're not trying to do everything yourself. They sometimes come back and thank me for pointing them in the right direction when I've referred them on to someone else.

It's impossible to pinpoint exactly which aspect of GPs' work causes the most stress – it's probably different for every one of us – but it seems to me that our involvement with, and responsibility for, other people, the element of the job which many of us find so rewarding, can also be our undoing. An enthusiastic GP begins his career keen to maintain good medical standards, increase his knowledge and skills, and build good relationships with patients. He must give a great deal of himself in time, energy and compassion if he is to achieve those goals. The workload, long hours, and time pressures are all stressful, and the GP also has to cope with considerable emotional demands which inevitably arise when caring for the sick.

For some doctors the strain becomes too much and they 'burn out'. The term, popularised in the United States, implies a loss of concern for patients due to job-related stress or 'psychological withdrawal from work in response to excessive stress and dissatisfaction'.[4] While researching this book I spoke to several doctors who had experienced burn-out, and had quit general practice to work in other areas of medicine as a result. Dr Max Turnbull was one of them; after more than 16 years as a GP, he left his practice to become a regional medical officer with the Department of Health.

'The job had become a nightmare'

It wasn't easy to leave general practice. I had no job to go to and I had to mortgage my home, but it was worth it. The job had become a nightmare. The practice was a big one and it was very busy. I was seeing 50 to 60 patients with appointments each day, plus extras put in as emergencies. When we moved into a health centre it became unbearable because we were so accessible. We were opposite the bus station so when everyone came into town shopping they'd pop in to the doctors too. Some of them seemed to live on our doorstep. I was going home every night at about half seven, absolutely knackered and often irritable, which took its toll on my wife and kids. My wife left home twice because she couldn't stand it, and my daughter ran away once as well.

4. O'Dowd, T. C., 'To burn out or rust out in general practice', *Journal of the Royal College of General Practitioners*, 1987; vol. 37, pp. 290–1.

My quality of life's improved now that I'm out of general practice.
I'm much more relaxed. After the stress of being a GP, my new job
makes me feel as if I'm permanently in a holiday camp.

Dr Dorothy McDowell left her practice in East Anglia at the
age of 53 after 26 years as a GP.

'I just dried up'

When I first started in practice in 1961 it was great. I worked
full-time and brought up four children too. Then four or five years
ago every day started to become a burden; I'd wake up each
morning and think gloomily, Not another day at work. I began to
not like the patients and even thought I might kill them.

Part of the problem was the feeling that patients just kept on
and on coming, and I couldn't stop them. I think the patients
thought that because I'm a woman I must be softer and would
listen endlessly to their problems, so I got landed with all the
ones who whinged and whined. I think people got dependent on
me and because I was reluctant to hand out pills, they used *me*
as their tranquilliser. In the end I think I just dried up on the milk
of human kindness.

The other part of the problem was the extended days and
weeks I had to work. I could just about cope with the eight a.m.
to six p.m. day but doing nights and weekends on call on top of
that was awful. People have become more demanding over the
last ten years and patients now expect doctors to be available all
the time. They would call at night for the most petty and trivial
things – I could count on my fingers the number of genuine
emergencies I saw in my last year in general practice.

Since I gave up general practice I've kept busy doing sessions
in a family planning clinic and that's great. Friends tell me I look
as if a great burden has been lifted from my shoulders – and it has.

Several characteristics were common amongst the burnt-out
GPs I spoke to. Many used terms such as 'ultra-conscientious',
'obsessive' or 'perfectionist' to describe themselves, and from
subjective accounts of their work timetable and medical commitments they did indeed seem to be doctors who aimed for high
standards in their work. Most expressed a strong sense of duty

towards patients and felt guilty if they could not solve their problems for them. Some put so much time and energy into work that they had little left over for family and their marriages suffered as a result.

Most of the doctors had been enthusiastic, at least initially, about general practice but found that, by dint of personality, they had attracted many patients with social, emotional and psychosomatic problems which rarely seemed to improve despite their attempts to provide practical help and support. In the end, many of these GPs felt unable to cope with the endless stream of problems brought to them, but also found it extremely difficult to ask for help themselves. They were afraid of being 'criticised', 'found out' and 'seen to be imperfect' and so struggled on alone, becoming more and more resentful of patients and the role they were expected to play for them.

For many GPs, finding the balance between duty to others and duty to themselves is very difficult. As with any 'caring' profession, our work can be physically and emotionally draining and we have to permit ourselves sufficient relaxation and outside interests to recharge our batteries and maintain the energy necessary to help others. We also need to question the image to which we aspire. The GP who slogs himself mercilessly may be a hero to his patients, but what good is a hero if he crumbles under the strain of living up to his public face?

An extra hidden burden that every GP must carry is the knowledge that his mistakes could hurt, or, even worse, kill, a patient. Humans are fallible and we accept that people make errors, but the GP cannot console himself with the thought that only money or credibility will be lost as a result of his mistakes. Instead, there is the very real possibility of cost in human terms. I will never forget an elderly lady I saw one Saturday night complaining of headache and a pain in her ear. She had an obvious ear infection and I thought her headache was part and parcel of this. I felt a little uneasy about her though, so asked her family to let me know if the headache worsened. A few hours later they phoned to say the pain was much more severe and when I examined the lady a second time it was clear that she had meningitis as well as the ear infection. Fortunately, I was able to get her into hospital immediately, where she responded well to treatment and survived, but I shudder whenever I think of the incident because my delay in diagnosing the meningitis could have cost the woman her life.

The prospect of making a fatal error is a nightmare for any doctor, but particularly so for a GP who is likely to know the patient and family well. Disasters are thankfully few and far between, but this weighty responsibility for other human beings never leaves us, and it causes every GP his share of sleepless nights and troubled days. Because patients in Great Britain are becoming more litigious, GPs are also aware that an error, or deficiency in the service they provide, is increasingly likely to give rise to complaints or legal action. This also adds to the burden of responsibility we carry, as Dr Angela Leigh described:

'You have the stress of being totally responsible'

As a GP you have the stress of being totally responsible for the patients you see, and that doesn't end at any point. Even if they go into hospital they become your responsibility again as soon as they're home. So you have to shoulder this total responsibility which carries the risk, unfortunately growing nowadays, of complaints. I think our practice has been fortunate on the whole because we've had very few, but the one or two we have had have been very traumatic.

The trouble is that when patients are dissatisfied it's often because they don't understand what general practice is all about. They see themselves coming to the surgery and perhaps having to wait, and they don't realise that that's because someone else has presented a problem that you can't just dismiss in the usual six minutes. You've got to deal with it there and then, which inevitably means other people will have to wait. The same thing goes for night calls – some people think they should be seen straight away. A lot of people do not consider others – they just think of themselves and what they want.

I think the greatest stress in general practice is when you've got two or more calls to go to all at once, and you've got to decide which of those is the one you need to go to first. You may not make the right decision and then you've got the stress of wondering if the patient or family will make a complaint. That, I think, is the very worst thing about general practice.

Despite work-related stress, job satisfaction is generally high amongst GPs. A study published by the Policy Studies Institute in 1988 [5] revealed that 84 per cent of GPs were very satisfied or satisfied with their job (compared with less than 60 per cent of hospital consultants). GPs were also more likely than consultants to cite subjective criteria, such as enjoying their job and the lifestyle it offered, as a measure of career success. A GP has more chance than a hospital doctor of being able to choose where in the country he will live, and the type of practice he will work in; he also reaches his maximum earning potential much earlier than his hospital colleagues. Nowadays, most young GPs will be earning a full share of their practice's profits three years after they are accepted as a partner. This means that GPs in their early thirties can expect to be making at least £30,000 (and in many cases considerably more), which is no doubt another factor boosting job satisfaction.

The elation I felt when I entered general practice stemmed from my discovery that it was possible to enjoy the intellectual challenge of medicine without losing sight of the patients whose problems I find so interesting. The opportunity to build a relationship of trust with patients over months or years is immensely satisfying for me. It is liberating in some ways too; just as a patient becomes more 'real' to me the better I know them, the more I think I become a 'real' person, and not just a doctor-figure, for them, when we have a chance to become well acquainted. Part of me is undoubtedly ambivalent about my doctor 'label', for in order to live up to the mythical images associated with it, I sometimes feel pressured into acting out a role rather than simply being myself. With the benefit of time and a good relationship with a patient, such role-playing becomes unnecessary because trust develops between us at a human, as well as a professional, level.

Finding the right approach for each patient is no easy task, for different people expect different things from their medical advisors. Some doctors (in hospital as well as general practice) are masters at using facets of their own personality to provide

5. Allen, I., *Any Room at the Top? A Study of Doctors and Their Careers*, Policy Studies Institute, London, 1988; p. 68.

the kind of doctoring that individual patients want; they do not pretend to be something they're not, but are sensitive to the individual's needs and so draw on the parts of themselves which that person will feel most comfortable dealing with.

An elderly GP I once worked for was obviously skilled in this art. Several of his patients told me how kind he was, and how ready he was to chat to them at length about their problems. Another of his patients, a rather stiff ex-army man, was equally enamoured of the doctor, but praised his 'direct, no-nonsense approach' which he felt had forced him to come to terms with his severe arthritis. That doctor was obviously capable of being both sympathetic and authoritarian, but knew exactly which approach would be most helpful to individual patients.

While GPs certainly do not have a monopoly on such skills, we are usually in a position to offer patients care which extends over months or years, which can embrace physical, psychological, social, emotional and sexual problems, and can cater for the healthy as well as the sick person. Our position as providers of primary care gives us the opportunity to become familiar with patients and, one hopes, as a result, to communicate well with them. People who find their doctor unhelpful, disinterested, and difficult to relate to, may scoff at the notion that GPs are capable of any such thing, and such criticism makes it clear that we still have a long way to go before we can claim to be satisfying the majority of our customers.

I do, however, feel sure that general practitioners have the potential to provide the personal element of medical care which hospital staff are finding it increasingly difficult to give patients. Your GP may not have the expertise of a specialist, nor the equipment and technical skills on offer from hospital, but he is likely to provide the one continuous thread running through your health care. Don't underestimate the value of his ongoing involvement with you and your life; it could be the single most important factor in securing the kind of individualised medical care you want.

CHAPTER 5

PREGNANCY AND BIRTH

THE ROLE OF medical care in pregnancy and childbirth has altered dramatically since the Second World War, and public reaction to that changing role has been both appreciative and critical. Improved standards of antenatal care contributed to lowering of maternal and infant death rates, to everyone's relief, but increasing levels of medical intervention during labour caused considerable distress to some women and resulted in a forceful movement demanding a return to 'natural' childbirth.

The debates over high-tech versus low-tech births, hospital versus home deliveries, and active versus passive labour have continued for many years; although changes have been effected more slowly than many women would have liked, there is no doubt that in this instance the consumer's voice was heard loud and clear, with the result that policies in many hospitals' delivery suites have become more flexible to try and give women a greater say in how their labour is managed.

Although women's views on childbirth received considerable media attention, less was heard from the doctors employing the technology which so many women resented. As pressure on hospital antenatal clinics has increased, so have the complaints about the service provided.

These are a sample of criticisms I heard from women at one London hospital antenatal clinic:

I've seen so many different midwives and doctors who all give me different advice, that now I'm thoroughly confused.

All the waiting seems such a waste of time. I sit here for hours then only get to see a doctor or midwife for a few minutes.

I dread having to come to the clinic because I have to bring my three-year-old son too and there's nowhere for him to play. He always ends up crying and I end up cross and tense.

As these comments suggest, long waiting times, crowded out-patient areas, poor facilities and impersonal treatment by the professionals have all been loudly criticised, yet again little has been heard from the doctors who staff these clinics and who, along with midwives, undertake a large proportion of the country's antenatal care. Although, not unnaturally, public concern over Britain's obstetric services has focused mainly on the needs of consumers, doctors (and midwives) have also been affected by changes in obstetric care. They too are frustrated and dissatisfied about some aspects of the service, and it is important to understand the difficulties they experience since their problems have important repercussions on the quality of care provided for pregnant women.

Pregnancy and childbirth produce enormous changes in a woman's life – physically, emotionally and socially. They also signal changes in the objectives of medical care. Pregnancy is not an illness (although some people treat pregnant women as invalids!) so doctors are not dealing with a disease, prescribing treatment and hoping for a cure. If complications arise, doctors may find themselves caring for a sick patient, but most women remain healthy throughout pregnancy and so, for them, the doctor's role is to keep a watchful eye and make sure that everything proceeds smoothly to a successful outcome.

Although pregnancy is not a disease it brings a woman into contact with doctors and other health professionals more frequently than if she had a chronic illness. Women receiving antenatal care throughout the whole of their pregnancy can expect to be seen by doctors or midwives 10 to 15 times, a level of medical attention which is unprecedented for most of them. For some this medical input is reassuring; for others it produces more anxiety than it relieves, because the very need for a doctor's involvement serves as a constant reminder that the pregnancy could go wrong. Linda Armstrong, a sales rep in her mid-twenties, had mixed feelings about her antenatal care:

'It made me nervous'

I was surprised at how many people saw me during the pregnancy – there was my G P, the health visitor, the hospital doctors and several midwives. I was quite flattered, I suppose, that being pregnant seemed to get me so much attention. But it also made me a bit nervous, especially towards the end, when I was being seen every week and had to keep a chart of the baby's movements, because it brought it home to me that something could suddenly go wrong and the baby might die.

Whatever a woman's reaction to this regular medical monitoring, the care she receives throughout pregnancy and labour does provide her with an opportunity (in theory at least) to become familiar with a number of health professionals as well as the hospital, clinic or GP surgery in which they work.

Several different doctors may contribute to a woman's obstetric care. A GP, consultant obstetrician and numerous junior hospital doctors may all play a part, and more may become involved if problems develop which require other specialist opinions. The kind of relationship that a woman will be able to build with any one doctor (or midwife) depends, in part, on the kind of antenatal care she receives. To understand why this is so, you need to know something of the different systems in operation throughout the country.

Most women are cared for during pregnancy and labour under one of three main schemes: hospital care, 'shared' care and GP obstetric (GPO) care. With hospital care, all routine medical checks take place in a hospital antenatal clinic, conducted by midwives, junior doctors and the consultant in charge. The woman gives birth in a hospital delivery suite, and although hospital midwives and doctors will certainly be in attendance during her labour, there is no guarantee that they will be the same staff she already knows from the antenatal clinic. Under the shared-care system, a consultant obstetrician again takes ultimate responsibility for the management of a woman's pregnancy and labour, although most of her antenatal checks are carried out by the GP, with infrequent visits to the hospital clinic. The baby is delivered in hospital, with staff there supervising the labour.

The major drawback to the hospital and shared-care schemes is the poor continuity of care they provide. At every hospital visit a woman may see a different doctor or midwife, preventing her from developing a good rapport with any of the staff. Does that really matter? Miss Carol Roylance, the forthright consultant obstetrician and gynaecologist at a London teaching hospital, had her doubts:

'Do patients find continuity important?'

Do patients find continuity very important? I personally don't think it is. I'm loath to say it because I know it's a popular concept that everyone should want to strive for continuity of care, but what happens if you get left to see the same midwife time after time and you don't like her, or she's got B.O., or you don't think she's right? Then continuity of care has backfired and you would much rather see someone else for a change. Just as I like seeing different patients and can't bear seeing the same patient over and over again, I think patients sometimes benefit from having a new brain on the problem, someone new to think about things.

Miss Roylance may feel that continuity isn't all it's cracked up to be, but a mountain of evidence suggests that pregnant women think otherwise. In 1983, *Parents* magazine received nearly 7,500 replies to their birth survey. The results showed that 'mothers would like antenatal, delivery and postnatal care to be provided, as far as possible, by the same people. Again and again, letters expressed the anxiety that arises when seeing a different doctor at each visit to the antenatal clinic, and at being delivered by total strangers – sometimes two different shifts of total strangers if a woman had a long labour. Continuity of care to the postnatal period might also have helped to reduce the frequent dissatisfaction with postnatal care.'[1]

1. Durward, L., 'Birth in Britain', a British *Parents* special report, November 1983.

In 1986, *Parents* magazine published the results of what they claimed to be 'the biggest ever national survey of women's feelings about maternity care'. The report concluded that 'good communications between parents and medical staff were helped where women saw the same doctor and midwife regularly. This was common among women who had their babies at home or in GP units but most mothers saw different people at almost every antenatal visit and were delivered by total strangers. While full of praise for the care they received, many women wished they could have had more continuity of care through pregnancy and beyond.'[2]

In its 1987 document 'Antenatal Care: Still Waiting for Action', the Association of Community Health Councils for England and Wales reported on several surveys carried out by CHCs exploring consumer satisfaction with antenatal care. Kidderminster CHC found that women 'complained about seeing different doctors on different occasions, so being required to explain their whole medical background etc. on each visit'. A 1982 Plymouth CHC survey found that '80 per cent of women did not see the same consultant on each visit to the clinic and 73 per cent did not see the same midwife. However, 77 per cent of women reported that they would have liked to have seen the same staff.' West Birmingham CHC asked women how they thought that continuity would affect their care. 'The women reported that they felt that the quality of care would be improved by doctors becoming familiar with individual cases and having an overview of the development of the pregnancy. The women expressed irritation that the consultants often appeared reliant on notes made by other doctors and often repeated questions. The women also said that if they could get to know their consultants a little they would feel less inhibited about asking questions.'

If continuity is so important to pregnant women, why is it rarely provided by hospital antenatal clinics? One of the reasons is the sheer volume of women to be seen, compared with the number of consultants available to look after them. With large numbers of women assigned to every consultant, much of the

2. Durward, L., 'Birth: 9000 mothers speak out', British *Parents*, November 1986.

work in antenatal clinics must be done by junior doctors, who are often forced to change jobs every six months in order to fulfil training requirements. Mr Malcolm Whittington, who had been a consultant in the west of England for 11 years, told me about the problem.

'A lot of my patients I never see'

We have four consultants in obstetrics and gynaecology at this hospital, for a population of about 400,000. Now, if you went to a place like Adelaide in Australia they've got a population of just over a million, I think, and 110 obstetricians. If you convert the figures it means we should have 35 to 40 consultants here, so you can see the difference. A lot of my patients I might never see at all, and some of them say, 'Oh, I was under Mr Whittington, but of course I never saw him.' You hear patients say this, as if to say, 'You know, it's not a very good service is it?' But if they realised just how many patients we have under our care – and remember half my work's gynaecology – they might begin to see why.

Workload problems like this have a great influence on the way consultants view their own role with regard to antenatal patients, as Mr Whittington explained:

About 1,200 or 1,300 women are booked under my care every year. It's an enormous workload. One of my main tasks is deciding which women can safely be booked with their GP, and I also get to see a few women in late pregnancy with problems. I think one sees one's role primarily as a troubleshooter. I accepted that that's the way it would be because that's the way it was in hospitals where I worked as an SHO and registrar. You realised consultants were fairly thin on the ground and they tended to oversee things and devote their skills where they were most needed, leaving the more routine things to their own junior staff and general practitioners.

Miss Roylance was in full agreement with this view of the consultant obstetrician's role:

'My role should be to teach'

I still go down to the clinic and I see some patients who are just normal women with normal pregnancies going through. And that's no bad thing. It's probably quite nice for them and quite nice for me, and nice to teach students on. But I think really my role should be to teach, and to see problem cases before the problems arise. I do think the role of a consultant should be to consult. I don't think the role of the consultant is to be another pair of hands in an antenatal clinic.

When I questioned Mr Stephen Payne, a young obstetrician and gynaecologist at a teaching hospital in the north-east Midlands, he also acknowledged how difficult it is for consultants to provide continuity and personal care for the majority of their patients. I asked him if he thought his role as a consultant was to provide an overview of patients' treatment, or personal care:

'Ideally it's both'

Ideally it's got to be both of those but I'm acutely aware of the fact that one provides personal care for a relatively small proportion of the patients coming through. In the majority, unfortunately, one is subserving the other role, a rather more impersonal one, of just providing an overview and carrying the can. It's the former of those roles that I would like to achieve, but in practice it's the second for the majority I'm sure. It can't change with the number of patients there are. The only way of changing it is by increasing consultant numbers and decreasing the number of patients in the clinic.

Although changes like these would appeal to many women receiving antenatal care, several consultants were concerned that medical training would suffer if patient numbers were reduced and consultants, rather than itinerant junior doctors, were to do most of the routine antenatal work. The junior doctors would then get little experience in antenatal care and, as Mr Payne remarked, 'It's fine saying the consultant will see only 12 patients in an afternoon and nobody's going to see an

SHO, but it makes the SHO a pretty useless consultant when his day comes.'

With the numbers of consultant obstetricians at their current levels, and with most of them employed to provide both gynaecology and obstetric services, antenatal clinics could not function without other doctors helping out. Unfortunately, some women feel cheated if they don't see the consultant during their pregnancy or after the birth, and although their disappointment is understandable it is often a reflection of their own well-being and the consultant's busy timetable, rather than any lack of care on his part. Miss Roylance explained the problem:

'I'm involved when anything goes wrong'

I don't think it's an indictment of our service when a patient says, 'I was booked under Miss Roylance and I never saw her.' I think that means that everything must have gone smoothly and it wasn't necessary for me to be involved. Because certainly I am involved whenever anything starts to go wrong or when there's a particularly difficult case.

Let me give you an outline of how I spend a week, because it shows the amount of other things I have to do apart from attending antenatal clinics. At 7.30 a.m. on a Monday morning I operate on private patients, drop in quickly to my rooms in Harley Street, before coming on to the hospital and picking up the correspondence here. Then I go to a gynaecology–pathology meeting and spend the afternoon doing urodynamic studies on patients. After that I deal with urgent correspondence and sometimes see junior doctors who have problems that need advice of some sort. I usually leave work at about 7.30 or 8 p.m.

On Tuesday I get up at 5.30 in order to see the private patients I've operated on the previous day before teaching some doctors at 7.30. At 8.30 I do a teaching ward round on the labour ward then I drive down to the other hospital where I work, go into the antenatal clinic at ten o'clock, do a teaching round on both obstetric wards, then go back to the antenatal clinic to see any patients who've been kept to see me. I spend the afternoon operating on gynaecology patients and on Tuesday evening, as I'm on call anyway, I sit down with my research registrar and deal with his work. I spend the night in a flat opposite the hospital because my home's too far away. I'm often called, not

necessarily to come in, but for advice. I'm also on call at
weekends, usually about once in every five or six weekends.
Wednesday I spend all day in private practice[3] but I do drop in
at the hospital to see any patients I've operated on who need to
see me. On a Thursday I start my teaching round on the gynae
side at eight o'clock. Then I do gynae out-patients clinic all
morning and gynae operating theatre all afternoon. Every alternate
week I have video review sessions on a Thursday after work and
on the other weeks there are often research meetings here. On a
Friday I start a teaching round on the antenatal ward at 8.15 and
then I do the antenatal clinic all morning. Then there's a desperate
scrabble to try and get to the lunchtime meeting. After that I try
and get all the correspondence from the week done and finish up
any bits of administration before I leave and go out in the
evening. In addition there are of course a lot of committee
meetings that have to be fitted in. So it's actually an incredibly
busy working week.

With such wide-ranging duties to be executed, obstetricians
like Miss Roylance can hardly be blamed for not providing
continuity for the hundreds, even thousands, of women who
pass through their clinics every year, yet it is important that
those women should be able to build a trusting relationship
with *someone* caring for them during pregnancy and childbirth.
Can other hospital doctors fill the void? Unfortunately it seems
not, at least while the medical career training structure continues as it is at present.

Junior doctors are employed in obstetrics at SHO, registrar
and senior registrar level. Virtually all those at the latter two
grades will be training with a view to a career in obstetrics and
gynaecology. Some of the SHOs will also be planning a career
in 'obs and gynae' but quite a few will do just one six-month
post in the specialty, as part of their basic training for general
practice. Regardless of long-term career plans, an SHO post
usually lasts only six months and a registrar job a year, after
which the doctor must go on to another training post, a move
which often entails switching to a different hospital and sometimes another area of the country.

3. Miss Roylance was employed in her NHS post for nine sessions every week, as opposed to the 11
sessions that full-time consultants are contracted for. This meant she was able to spend two sessions
(equivalent to a full day) each week in private practice.

93

As there are no housemen in obstetrics (because the specialty cannot provide the broad medical and surgical experience they need in the pre-registration year), SHOs are the most junior doctors on an obstetrics firm. Their jobs are often exceptionally busy, for they must do the routine ward work of a houseman, attend antenatal clinics, supervise patients' postnatal care and do spells of duty on the delivery suite. Those whose job also entails work in gynaecology must assist in the operating theatre, look after patients on the gynaecology wards and help in the out-patient clinics as well. The workload reduced me to tears on occasions when I was an SHO, and several of the young doctors I met also found the work backbreaking. Dr Jenny Scott was a GP trainee who had done six months in obstetrics:

'I felt like death warmed up'

The obstetrics was very, very hard work with ridiculous hours. I did a one-in-two rota for two months, then a one-in-four for four months. When I was on from Friday morning through to Monday I'd often only get nine or ten hours' sleep in total, so by Monday I was a complete wreck. There wasn't enough cover really. Not enough people around when there was more than one problem to be dealt with. At weekends there'd be one SHO and one registrar covering 60 patients. I lost nine pounds in weight and felt like death warmed up.

SHOs beginning their first post in obstetrics are often nervous at the prospect. Although it's usually several years since they studied the subject at medical school, from the first day of the job they will be expected to assess patients in the antenatal clinics and take some responsibility for women in labour. Dr Karen Underhill, a gentle 28-year-old SHO planning to become a GP, spoke about her feelings before she started her obstetrics job:

'Something terrible was going to happen'

I was looking forward to it in some ways but I was also quite frightened because it's a difficult specialty and the juniors seem to be expected to do a lot and yet you also have an awful lot to

learn. I was terrified of what might happen on the delivery suite.
To a certain extent that stayed with me throughout the job. I
always had a fear that something terrible was going to happen
and I was going to be responsible.

Everything about the SHOs' work militates against them providing the continuity that women need during pregnancy and labour. With each post lasting only six months there are very few women whom they will be able to follow through the entire pregnancy. Even when they can, it is often deemed wise for other more senior doctors to see the women periodically to make sure that the relatively inexperienced SHO has not missed a significant problem. Continuity is made more difficult by the SHO's sometimes irregular attendance at clinics; if an urgent problem arises on the ward or delivery suite, or if it is his day to deal with emergency admissions, he may be called away from the clinic and so the women who already know him may have to see another, unfamiliar, face. The doctors' heavy workload can itself encourage a mechanical and apparently insensitive approach to patients, for when they're tired and rushed off their feet they're less likely to spend time answering questions and giving the explanations and reassurance that pregnant women often need. Karen Stanley, from Kent, had found this a problem in the busy antenatal clinic she attended:

‘Clinics were a cattle market’

The clinics were more like a cattle market than anything else.
Women being herded in and out of rooms as quickly as possible.
I suppose the doctors and midwives were under a lot of pressure
with so many women to see but I still wish they could've taken a
bit more time to answer my questions. One doctor made me feel
a real nuisance because I asked him about a new form of pain
relief in labour and I felt like telling him, 'It's me who's got to
push this baby out you know.'

Being unable to provide personal care is a problem which produces different reactions in different junior doctors; some feel guilty, while others become concerned with their own needs at the expense of the patients'.

'I wasn't talking to them'

DR JENNY SCOTT: I felt very dissatisfied with some of my jobs.
You were so busy. You had to clerk in all these people and sort
out the problems, but you didn't have the time to talk to them
and you knew they were terribly anxious and uptight. To make
time for them and their relatives was difficult. Obstetrics was the
worst because, well, it's supposed to be such a good experience
for the woman, having a baby. I felt guilty that I wasn't spending
time talking to them, and guilty that no one else was either. Not
having time to talk to people was one of the worst stresses of
the job. I wouldn't say that happened *all* the time, but an awful
lot of the time. It's such a shame, it should have been a really
nice experience, but I'm afraid I didn't enjoy the job at all.

Dr Janet Rodgers, a 27-year-old SHO in obstetrics and gynaecology, was finding life as a junior doctor much tougher than
she'd anticipated. The fact that she felt no one really cared
about *her* problems clearly made it difficult for her to sympathise
with patients' problems at times.

'I can't spend time with them'

GR: When you're tired does it influence how much you talk to
patients, how sympathetic you are?

DR JANET RODGERS: Definitely. Especially when you've got women
coming in for terminations or who've had miscarriages. It
becomes so commonplace to have women miscarrying when
they're 10 to 12 weeks' pregnant. You say to them 'Well, you
know, one in four pregnancies goes this way and I'm sorry, it's
just the way it's gone for you and you need a D. and C. so let's
take you to theatre.' If you're busy and you've got emergencies
on the delivery suite – with babies who are viable – then you've
just got to get on. You hope that the nurses will take over where
you left off and will explain things more fully to the woman and
spend time speaking to her and dealing with the emotional
aspects. We just don't have time.

GR: Do you worry about that?

DR JANET RODGERS: I don't. I don't think I do worry about it
because I'm doing the best I can. If I'm only getting two hours'

sleep a night I think I'm really doing as much as I can. I can't spend any more time with the patients, I really can't. If it's a quietish day and somebody comes in who's emotionally upset then I will spend time with them, but by and large I just can't.

If junior doctors provide little in the way of personal care for women during pregnancy, they often manage even less during childbirth. Historically, it has been midwives who stay with women during labour, and when hospital obstetrics took over from community care this pattern continued, for uncomplicated deliveries at least. Junior doctors working on a delivery suite are not assigned to individual women as midwives are. Instead they tend to be called in to perform specific tasks such as putting up drips or stitching episiotomies. Midwives take responsibility for normal deliveries but if problems arise they are duty bound, under midwifery regulations, to summon a doctor for help or advice.

Dividing responsibilities between midwives and doctors in this way has significant consequences both for the staff and for labouring women. It sometimes creates an awkward working relationship between midwives and junior doctors, especially SHOs with little obstetric experience. They often find themselves being called in to 'advise' midwives who have infinitely more knowledge about how to manage problems during labour. Doctors who've grown accustomed to giving orders to nurses may feel very uncomfortable when the tables are turned and they find midwives telling them what to do. Both sides may be guilty of 'pulling rank' and even if they manage a truce between them it is often only an uneasy one. Dr Peter Rosser, an Australian doctor working as an obstetrics SHO in North Wales, told me:

'There's a lot of one-upmanship'

The politics of doctors against midwives upset me at first, and seems to be a common experience amongst SHOs. There's certainly a lot of one-upmanship between junior doctors and midwives, particularly in the first few months when you're settling in. You find you're being told what to do by the nursing staff much more than you're used to in any other job. I consider myself a fairly easy-going and broad-minded sort of person but it was really getting to me.

'I cried for hours'

DR KAREN UNDERHILL: Getting on with some of the midwives was very hard. Some of them were really nice and could tell you what to do tactfully, but others would embarrass you in front of the patients. I can remember one occasion, it was quite early on in the job when i was still finding my feet and lacked confidence, and it was also at the end of a weekend on call when I was very tired. A midwife was so rude to me in front of a patient that I rang my husband and said 'I'm leaving! I'm resigning tomorrow!' and I cried about it for hours.

Cathy Penrose, a midwife at a London hospital, put forward her point of view:

'They treat me as a skivvy'

I know it must be difficult for some SHOs being thrown in at the deep end on the labour ward when they first start the job, but it can be very irritating for midwives having to call them in when you're worried about a patient, only to have them stand around looking clueless. Even worse than that are the ones who think they know it all and just treat me as some kind of skivvy who's there to run around after them. If they want me to respect them as a doctor they should show some respect for my training and experience in midwifery.

The way responsibility during childbirth is shared between doctors and midwives also has important implications for the way doctors relate to women in labour. Although all the staff may be strangers to a woman when she first arrives on the delivery suite, one midwife will stay with her during her labour (or at least for the duration of her eight-hour shift) and so has a chance to get to know the woman and her partner. The doctor's main role is to assess and deal with any problems as they arise, so he may not meet the woman until she is well advanced in labour. Because the baby is often thought to be in danger, the doctor may have to make decisions and take practical action quickly, without any chance to build a rapport with the woman involved. Sarah Mills, who needed to have a Caesarian because her baby became distressed during labour, had found this quite upsetting:

'He only talked to the midwife'

I was getting on really well in labour, with my husband and the midwife giving me lots of encouragement, when suddenly the baby's heart started to slow down. The doctor was called in and seemed very worried. He only talked to the midwife and not to my husband or me, so I didn't really understand what had gone wrong. Then he said I'd have to have a Caesarian immediately and I didn't know what to think. I'd never seen him before, but there he was saying it had to be a Caesarian. I was so worried for the baby that I didn't argue but I wished he'd been someone I knew, then at least I would've been able to trust his judgement.

As a junior doctor I found this kind of emergency intervention a very uncomfortable situation to deal with; however necessary the action might seem, I still felt an intruder on what is obviously to most couples, a very personal and emotional event. When I spoke to a number of junior doctors who had experienced similar circumstances I was surprised to find only a couple who had felt as I had. Dr Karen Underhill was one of them:

'You felt a complete stranger'

It could be difficult, particularly if you were called in towards the end of the labour, for a forceps delivery or something like that, you could feel a bit of an intruder because the midwife knew the patient but you didn't. Sometimes you didn't know the mother at all, and you felt a complete stranger, yet you had to walk in and start fiddling around with her most intimate parts. That was very difficult.

Other doctors, like Dr Ingrid Goedt from Germany, found no real problems intervening in the labour room:

No, I don't feel awkward because if something needs doing, it needs doing. Anyway, diplomacy is not one of my fortes. So I just go in and say, 'Hello, I'm Dr Goedt, I'm the SHO on call,' and do what needs doing.

I found just as much variation in junior doctors' emotional response to childbirth. Karen Underhill and Ingrid Goedt were again good examples of opposite ends of the spectrum:

DR KAREN UNDERHILL: Sometimes I do get worked up at a birth. Several times I felt tears pricking the back of my eyes when the baby was born and yes, I was comfortable showing how I felt. I think it's a very good thing to show that you can sympathise and that you're happy with the parents.

DR INGRID GOEDT: Initially I got emotionally involved at the birth but not any more. Now the novelty has worn off. I always try to force myself to grin and say 'Congratulations' but even that's very hard sometimes if I've been called out of bed for the fifth time that night.

Although several of the SHOs I spoke to remained distanced and detached from the majority of women they dealt with during labour, virtually all of them became much more involved with any woman who experienced a stillbirth or neonatal death. Despite being very moved by such tragedies, the doctors found it difficult to reveal their feelings to patients. They became extremely uncomfortable when their own emotions threatened to disturb their composed professional image.

'There's no point blubbering'

DR JANET RODGERS: When someone comes in with a stillborn baby it's awful because the couple have been waiting nine months for a happy event and all of a sudden everything's thrown back in their face. Sometimes I don't know how to cope with that. I mean quite often I have to leave the room because I know that if I stayed I'd burst into tears.

GR: Would you find that difficult to do, to show a patient your feelings?

Dr Janet Rodgers: Yes, because you have the impression that you're there to do a job and there's no point in standing there blubbering because that isn't helping them. I tend to try and find something else to do, like busy myself with sewing up the woman or making sure her blood pressure's OK. Something like that, something technical or practical, because that's a lot easier to cope with.

Sadly, Dr Rodgers' reaction is typical of most doctors. Trained to behave as strong, dependable individuals we are then frightened to admit to ourselves or our patients that we too can be affected emotionally by the human tragedies we have to deal with in the course of our work.

Dr Rodgers' efforts to hide her feelings probably made her appear brusque and rather uncaring to the couple involved, and although she believed that crying with them would have been unhelpful, grieving parents may feel otherwise. In a 1988 newsletter of the Stillbirth and Neonatal Death Society a mother whose baby son had died at birth expressed her gratitude to the medical staff who had not only cared, but had *showed* her that they cared:

'A few tears to shed'

The obstetric care I was given was excellent and I would simply like to say that there were caring medical people with just the right touch and just the right thought and most especially a few tears to shed over the loss of that precious boy. The greatest tribute paid to him was the attendance at his funeral service of both the registrar who delivered him and some of the midwifery staff. That, more than anything, spoke volumes of their love and concern for us and our firstborn child.

Doctors obviously need to learn that allowing themselves to be human, and be *seen* to be human, is a vital part of their role in childbirth. Women feel this most keenly when they have lost a baby, but it is necessary, to some extent, for *all* deliveries if doctors are to respond with sensitivity to women's emotional

101

needs during labour. Dr Tom Peterson, an astute and reflective GP, said of doctors:

'Objectivisation is part of the training'

They may not underestimate the emotional importance of pregnancy and childbirth to women, but they would often like to dodge it because it deals with areas of their emotions that they feel professionally they should have eliminated out of the 'objectivised' bit of themselves.

That objectivisation is part of the training of a scientific individual.

The need to maintain emotional detachment from patients seems to affect doctors most when the women they are dealing with are strangers. When doctors know the women well it helps them to become more relaxed and involved and to get greater satisfaction from their role in childbirth, so in this sense continuity has benefits for doctors as well as patients.

Unfortunately, with hospital care organised as it is at present, junior doctors and consultants can rarely develop with patients the kind of rapport that might help them both, so it is to the GP and midwives that we must look for continuity in maternity care.

With GPO care it is the general practitioner, rather than a hospital consultant, who takes ultimate responsibility for the woman's obstetric care. The GP and community midwives carry out all the antenatal checks and it is the GP, not a hospital doctor, who deals with any problems that arise during the delivery. Of course, not all births happen in hospital; a few women choose to deliver at home, and here again it is community midwives and GPs who supervise their care during pregnancy and labour.

The vast majority of GPs in Britain provide some antenatal services, usually on a shared-care basis with local hospitals. A much smaller number undertake GPO care because it entails responsibility for deliveries, and necessitates additional experience and skills which many GPs feel they do not have. Since a goodly proportion of babies are born at night or during a weekend it also means extra out-of-hours work for the doctor, and many GPs are reluctant to take on this duty in addition to their normal on-call commitment.

Lesley Hollingsworth, a 26-year-old mother from Newcastle-upon-Tyne, was certainly very grateful that her doctor offered GPO care:

'It was much more personal'

With my first baby I was under the hospital and it was all right. But with the second, my G P offered to do all the antenatal care and be at the delivery. It was so much nicer that way.

I got to know him and a couple of the local midwives very well during the pregnancy, and it was very reassuring when he popped into the hospital to see how things were going when I was in labour. All in all it was much more personal than my first pregnancy.

GPs who do choose to offer full obstetric care to their patients do so for a variety of reasons. Dr Stephen Kerr, the 61-year-old Oxfordshire GP, enjoyed many aspects of this obstetric work, especially the practical side.

'Keeps the adrenalin flowing'

I'm a practical sort of person. I'm happiest doing obstetrics or gynaecology or minor surgery. It's partly my training and partly my own personality – I'm a practical DIY man rather than a counsellor. Obstetrics is enjoyable because you're dealing with a healthy population by and large which makes a nice change, and you see such a lot of happiness usually as a result of it. I still think there's something a little bit magical about childbirth really. There's also a certain amount of drama, a certain amount of excitement – that all keeps the adrenalin flowing.

For other GPs the relationship they build with women during and after pregnancy is more interesting than the practical side of obstetrics.

'What is interesting is the person not the uterus'

DR TOM PETERSON: When I was doing hospital obstetrics, before I
became a GP, I realised I was really interested not in the science
of obstetrics but in the care aspect of obstetrics. I was trying to
do primary care in the wrong setting. I couldn't provide care for
people in their own environment. I knew I would enjoy obstetrics
more if I had an ongoing relationship with the women I was
delivering, rather than having to sever links with them just when
I was beginning to find out what made them tick. More and
more I've come to find that what is interesting is the person
'around' the baby and not the labouring uterus.

Dr Angela Leigh, the 61-year-old Midlands GP, also emphasised the importance of the relationships she developed with
women during pregnancy and birth. She saw complete antenatal
care as an integral part of her general practice work.

'General practice is about the family'

Obstetrics gives me an ideal opportunity for building relationships
with women. The patients that I know best in the practice are
those that I've antenataled. You build a very close relationship
through the antenatal period, the birth, and afterwards. General
practice is about the family – about being involved with the
family, and if you do full obstetric care you do get involved with
the whole family. The father is usually there at the birth, and you
see him when you visit the home, so you get to know them all. I
think being involved with the pregnancy and birth gives a
wholeness to the family's relationship with you as a GP.

Of the three common types of obstetric care, the GPO system
is the only one that can guarantee that a woman will see
familiar faces throughout her pregnancy, delivery and postnatal
period. Other schemes which aim to provide continuity of care
do exist but are offered routinely by only a few health auth-
orities. One such example is the 'Domino' scheme under which
almost all the antenatal care is provided by community
midwives, except perhaps for an occasional check by a GP or
consultant. One of the community midwives delivers the baby
in hospital and the woman is transferred home as early as six

hours after the birth for postnatal care from the community midwifery team. Schemes such as this, and GPO care, are undoubtedly popular with women for they promise the kind of personalised care that they want during pregnancy and childbirth. GPs who undertake full obstetric care recognise this ability to provide continuity for their patients as one of the great advantages of the service.

'The same person right through'

DR ANGELA LEIGH: Our GPO care is important because it gives women the opportunity to have the same people looking after them throughout the antenatal period, through delivery and postnatally and then we'll follow-up looking after the babies, rather than somebody seeing them antenatally, somebody totally different when they go into hospital and so on. The hospital system provides no continuity, but our community midwives go into hospital with some, though not all, of the women to deliver them, so there's a hope that the women will have the same person right through. It doesn't always work, because of off-duty rotas and so on, but there'a greater chance of them having continuity.

'A special relationship'

DR TOM PETERSON: If you offer GPO delivery, 85 per cent of women will take it, with only limited knowledge of how good you are at it. They seem to take it on trust. They seem to want not your skills but your personality. That's why the continuity of GPO care is important. I think women have a special relationship with the person who looks after them during pregnancy and birth because it's a very important time in their lives. Their first labour is a major test in their lives, a sort of test of womanhood.

Labour is indeed a testing time for women and some feel strongly that they need the familiar and secure environment of their own home to help them through the experience. Whereas 76 per cent of births took place at home in 1932, by the 1960s hospital deliveries accounted for 91.4 per cent of all births. The use of modern technology and the availability of skilled obstetricians was thought to make childbirth far safer in hospital than at home, and although several studies have since argued the benefits and safety of home delivery for certain low-risk groups of women, most GPs are still reluctant to take on the responsibility of a home birth.

While acknowledging how important a home delivery is to some women, I can understand a doctor's reservations about it, for I have supervised home births and know the anxiety that a GP feels, wondering if anything will go wrong. Our training tends to put emphasis on the possible complications of childbirth, and with a heightened awareness of these problems it is difficult for us not to fret over the safety of the mother and baby. Even experienced GP obstetricians worry that they might lack the skills or facilities to deal with a sudden emergency at home, and with the demise of obstetric flying squads in many areas, the GP knows there is no back-up service he can call on to provide swift help in the event of a serious problem. Several of the GPs I interviewed put forward their views on home deliveries.

'Not if I can help it'

GR: Do you do any home deliveries?

DR STEPHEN KERR: Not if I can help it. If a woman is adamant about it then the midwife legally has to attend her and my policy is that if the midwife has to take somebody on at home because they insist, then it's up to me to back my midwife up.

GR: Is there a flying squad available?

DR STEPHEN KERR: Well, it's really fallen into disuse through natural atrophy. The anaesthetist used to be the key man in the flying squad, either for resuscitation or for providing an anaesthetic if you had a surgical procedure to do, like removing a retained placenta, but nowadays the anaesthetists in many areas say 'We're not going out any more because we're more valuable in the hospital.' So if we run into any serious problems with a woman at home it has to be an ordinary ambulance to take her to hospital. But if you don't do any home obstetrics, you're not going to have that sort of problem.

GR: Do you get women tentatively asking about the possibility of home delivery?

Dr Stephen Kerr: Yes, and then we spend some time talking to them, trying to explain the advantages of hospital care and the fact that you cannot foresee every emergency in obstetrics. It helps that we have a very flexible policy in our GP unit. They can either stay six hours or 24 hours or 48 hours, or, if they're really wanting a holiday, they can stay a whole week there.

'I don't encourage them'

Dr Angela Leigh: I'm glad high-tech obstetrics exists but it's not necessary for everyone. A lot of our patients don't want it and we can offer them low-tech deliveries. We do a few home deliveries. Frankly, I don't encourage them because you don't know when something's going to go wrong, but we will undertake them under certain circumstances, and always with the understanding that if a problem does arise the woman will be prepared to go into hospital.

'Certain women need this'

Dr Tom Peterson: Looking at home confinement, I recognise that in the early part of my training certain factors created prejudices within me. Because my mother had a disastrous home confinement and there was also a prevailing tendency to eliminate home confinement as a facility nationally, I went along with this. Later in life I perceived that certain women genuinely had a need for this facility and, as a person who was a servant of a community, one actually needed to perceive and cater for their need by agreeing to a home delivery if they wanted one.

GPs are being asked to take on more and more medical care previously dealt with by hospital doctors and although it means an even greater workload, maternity service is another area where the advantages of community-based care seem to be enormous. Both GPs and community midwives can provide women with continuity during pregnancy, as well as during delivery and the postnatal period in some cases. For GPs, our role in a woman's pregnancy and delivery is not an isolated service, but part of our ongoing care of the whole family. I find antenatal work tremendously enjoyable and rewarding in itself;

as an added bonus the bond that develops between myself and a patient during maternity care undoubtedly pays dividends for both of us later on, when the woman, her baby, or other members of the family can receive medical help from a doctor they know and, I hope, trust.

Although 95 per cent of GPs offer antenatal and postnatal care, only about ten per cent actually deliver babies. Sadly, in the future there may be even fewer doing so, as medico-legal problems make GPs reluctant to take responsibility for care during labour. Fear of litigation over babies damaged at birth is scaring off some GPs, and if insurance rates are increased for those practising obstetrics (as has been threatened), even more will opt out of this kind of work. Deterrents like these won't affect GPs' care of women before and after delivery but will stop many of them offering their services during the crucial period of childbirth.

Sadly, if you are pregnant and unhappy with your current antenatal care there may be little you can do to improve the situation unless you're prepared to switch to an alternative system of care midway through the pregnancy. If you haven't yet opted for any particular scheme, it's worth thinking hard about what you want from medical care during pregnancy and labour. Find out from your GP or community midwife what types of antenatal care are available in your area and bear in mind that the system of care you choose (I'm assuming of course that you have a choice, which, unfortunately, isn't the case for all women) will play a big part in influencing the kind of relationship you have with the doctor(s) and midwives looking after you.

As for the services on offer to pregnant women, the uncertainty over the future of GP obstetrics makes it all the more important that the need to improve hospital maternity care is not ignored. Many hospitals are trying to reduce clinic waiting times, provide better facilities, and raise the standard of their service in other ways, but the provision of continuity, information and attention to individual needs depends to a large extent on adopting new systems of care which ensure that women will be seen by the same few members of staff, wherever possible, during pregnancy, childbirth and the postnatal period.

Such alternative systems have been tried and have worked successfully, at least on a small scale. *The 'Know Your Midwife' Report*,[4] for example, describes a scheme adopted from 1983 to 1985 at St George's Hospital, London, in which a team of four midwives gave care to women in the antenatal clinic, delivery suite and postnatal ward, ensuring that continuity was provided throughout all stages of maternity care. With the knowledge that such schemes can be both popular and effective, what we need now is for doctors, midwives, pregnant women and hospital administrators to understand one another's needs and problems, and together look for new ways to deliver hospital obstetric care. If we can also provide adequate training and incentives for GPs to undertake a fuller role in maternity care, we have the makings of a system which would benefit both the users and the providers of the service.

4. Flint, C., Poulengeris, P., *The 'Know Your Midwife' Report*, 1987. Copies from 49 Peckarmans Wood, London SE26 6RZ.

CHAPTER 6

SICK CHILDREN

MOST PARENTS KNOW only too well the difficulties and anguish to be faced when caring for a sick child. Lack of experience with medical problems leaves them feeling anxious about what they should do, and parental love and concern make it all the more painful to watch small children suffer. It might therefore seem reasonable to assume that doctors, both knowledgeable in medical matters and less emotionally involved with sick children than their parents, might find caring for youngsters an easy task. In fact, diagnosing and treating children's illnesses requires special skills and knowledge, and without these doctors may feel as nervous as any parent. Even with years of experience, caring for seriously ill children is a worrying business, for the lives of these tiny charges are so precious to their families that the responsibility for saving them weighs heavy on a doctor's shoulders.

In a medical sense, children cannot be considered as miniature adults. The symptoms and physical signs they develop as a result of a particular illness are often quite different from those found in adults with the same complaint. Meningitis, for example, causes headaches, photophobia (dislike of bright light) and a stiff neck in adults, but in babies may produce rather non-specific features such as irritability and vomiting. Not only are signs and symptoms in children frequently dissimilar to those in adults, but they often vary according to the child's age. A urinary tract infection could cause prolonged jaundice in a newly born baby, feeding problems or a fever in an older infant, and vague malaise or bedwetting in a school-age child. Not surprisingly, therefore, the medical care of children has developed into a separate specialty, paediatrics, requiring knowledge and expertise which in many ways are quite distinct from those needed in adult medicine.

110

All medical students spend some time during their training studying paediatrics. For most, the period is some six to ten weeks long; ample time for those intent on a career such as adult psychiatry or surgery, but not for those planning to work with children, as paediatricians or GPs. Doctors wanting to concentrate on paediatrics spend many years in specialist training posts after they qualify from medical school, and so become confident and competent in children's medical care. Some would-be GPs are not so lucky. Although they are encouraged to spend more time in paediatrics as part of their post-graduate training, appropriate hospital posts are often difficult to come by, so they may get little, or no, further experience with sick children before being faced with the responsibility of treating them in general practice. As a result, some young doctors find the prospect of ill youngsters very daunting. Dr Jenny Scott, the GP trainee from East London:

'I'd lie awake and worry'

I'm terrified of children dying. When I first started my trainee year I was so anxious about ill babies I'd seen and whether I'd missed something serious that I'd lie awake and worry about them, wondering whether I should have sent them into hospital or not. I think that's a natural anxiety and probably quite appropriate. It's got better since I've seen more babies. I think it was particularly worrying for me because I hadn't done any paediatrics after leaving medical school.

One of the basic principles that any doctor working with children has to learn is that dealing with a child means dealing with the family too. Parents can often contribute important information about the history of their child's illness, and if the child is very young it may be the only history available. A parent's presence may be vital security for a child during experiences which it finds frightening, like being examined by a doctor, having X-rays and blood tests, and staying in a vast and unfamiliar hospital ward. Parents may be essential in helping to administer and monitor children's treatment, particularly with a chronic (long-lasting) illness such as diabetes or epilepsy. Last,

111

but by no means least, parents and siblings may be far more anxious about the sick child than he is himself, so explanation and reassurance for the whole family is an important part of paediatric care. In this sense the family, rather than the child alone, becomes 'the patient'.

The triangular relationship between doctor, child and parent is sometimes difficult for all concerned. Margaret Clarke, a housewife in her mid-thirties whose ten-year-old daughter has asthma, described the problems she had experienced:

'I shouldn't interfere'

Carol hates being different from her friends so she often won't use her inhalers at school. I have to go down there every lunch break to make sure she's had her midday doses. Our GP seems to think I shouldn't interfere so much – he's told me more than once that Carol should be able to manage the asthma herself by now – but I know she wouldn't if I didn't nag her about it all the time.

I've been involved in situations like this one, where I've found it more difficult dealing with a parent than I have with their sick child, and it's easy to see why a degree of conflict sometimes develops between parents and a doctor. The problem often arises over the diagnosis, rather than management, of a child's illness. Mothers (and fathers for that matter) may feel intuitively that they know when something is wrong with their child even though a doctor can find nothing abnormal, and often they will be proved right. On the other hand, a parent's natural anxiety can colour their judgement about offspring, and a doctor's objective assessment may, in some instances, prove more accurate in pinpointing the problem. To draw conclusions about an individual child, a balance has to be struck between the specific and personal knowledge of the parents, and the more generalised medical knowledge of the doctor. Failure to do so can only lead to resentment and strife, neither of which do anything to help the ailing youngster.

Doctors are taught to diagnose illness according to familiar patterns of symptoms and signs (and may be disparaging about parental intuition), but years of experience may encourage them to rely less on paediatric textbooks and more on their own instincts. In fact, doctors sometimes develop a kind of 'sixth sense' about sick children, which is not unlike parents' intuitive understanding of their child. Some doctors can spot serious illness at a glance, without need of detailed history or physical examination. The diagnosis may be far from clear, but they will 'know it in their bones' that the child is very sick and in need of urgent treatment.

'A kind of sixth sense'

DR HENRY WINTERTON, THE WEST-COUNTRY GP: I think every GP who's been at it for any length of time certainly develops this kind of sixth sense. Oh yes, I think you get a sense of knowing when things aren't running a natural course, when something jars. It's little things that jar, like a child being too flushed, or sweating too much, or not enough, or lying too still or having pupils that are too big. I think you definitely do develop a special sense which tells you that something serious is going on.

Children's health, just like adults', is affected by more than purely physical factors. Poor housing, financial problems and disharmony within the family can affect a child's well-being just as much as measles or mumps. A GP who knows a family well is in an ideal position to discover whether a child's headaches or tummy pains are due to underlying physical or psychological problems. He must also gauge when a child's ailment is not the *real* problem at all. Some parents under stress repeatedly take their children to the doctor, too embarrassed or scared to ask for help for themselves; GPs have to be alert to the possibility that it is a parent, not the child they bring with them, who is really in need of attention. This sort of problem again brings it home that children cannot be treated in isolation from the family context, and emphasises the need for a good relationship between doctor, child and parents.

An interesting report from the Advertising Research Unit at the University of Strathclyde shows how difficult it can be for parents to build that kind of comfortable relationship with their family doctor.

Entitled 'Parents and the GP', the article is based on research carried out in Scotland in 1981, when 113 parents took part in small group discussions about various aspects of family life. The research revealed that some parents were reluctant to approach a professional, such as the GP, when they were worried about their children, either because they felt an outsider could not understand their problem or because asking for help made them feel that they had failed as parents. Once they had decided they needed medical help, the paper tells how

a number of parents described the decision of whether to actually obtain that help as lengthy and involved, and sometimes agonising. One of the main worries here was the feeling that the GP might feel they had asked for help in an arbitrary and thoughtless fashion. . . . Parents felt very conscious of the importance of 'not wasting the doctor's time'. They might feel guilty if they had called the doctor for an emergency visit and the child was 'running around' by the time he arrived, although both doctor and parents know that children can recover very quickly. One mother, with the heartfelt agreement of others in her discussion group, highlighted the irony:

'You almost give a sigh of relief when the doctor says the child is ill.'

Concern was also frequently expressed about being labelled as overanxious:

'I am sure he has me down as a fussing mother.'

Although far from flattering about GPs, I have to agree with the study's conclusions that 'The [parent's] fear is not imaginary. Such labels are used and do affect how the GP treats the parents' reports and how the child's condition is treated.' So why do GPs label some parents as overanxious? Usually because they take their children back and forth to the surgery, unable to cope with even minor illnesses on their own.

Lynn Downes, a 24-year-old single parent with a two-year-old son, Gary, told me how she went through a phase of taking him to the doctor every couple of weeks, and of the reaction she received:

'It's nothing serious'

I know I was down at the doctor's a lot but Gary never seemed
to be properly well. He had colds and temperatures, and coughs
that took ages to go away. The doctor always said 'It's nothing
serious' but I'd worry just the same. He didn't really tell me *why*
it wasn't serious, so I'd carry on worrying. And because I'm on
my own with Gary I felt if anything happened to him it'd be my
fault. I didn't tell the doctor that though. He wouldn't have
understood.

Lynn may have been right; perhaps her doctor wouldn't have
understood, but there's a chance he might, especially if he was
a parent himself. By not expressing her fears she made it easier
for the GP mentally to categorise her as a 'neurotic mother'
without thinking further about the reasons for her anxiety, and
about how he could reassure her. Every doctor needs clues from
parents so that he or she can address the particular worries
which are troubling them. Even then, you might still find it
difficult to believe what a doctor tells you, as did Geraldine
Sexton, the mother of four-year-old twins:

'I was so scared I took Paul to casualty'

When one of the twins got sick last winter I was really scared it
was meningitis. There'd been so much about it in the papers. He
had a temperature and a headache and everyone was saying that
headaches could be caused by meningitis. So I got the doctor
out and he said that Paul just had an ordinary virus and would
get better in a few days. I asked him how he could be so sure
and he said that despite the headache the other signs of
meningitis weren't there. I kept on thinking about what I'd read
though, and I was so scared that I took Paul up to the Casualty
Department a few hours later. The doctor there said the same
thing and wouldn't admit him. I was worried sick all weekend
but he did get better a few days later so I suppose the doctors
must've been right.

I suspect that if Mrs Sexton's GP had found out about her trip
to Casualty with Paul he would have felt annoyed, even insulted,
that she had not accepted his diagnosis and reassurance. Dr

Hilary Taylor, the 34-year-old London GP, described the kind of conflict which occasionally arose between herself and a parent when her efforts at reassurance failed:

'Parents ask for advice, then won't accept it'

I find it so frustrating when parents ask me for advice, then won't accept it. Take for instance when a mother phones me at night because her toddler's been feverish for a few hours. I realise she's probably anxious so I'll try to reassure her and I'll ask lots of questions in order to be clear in my own mind whether the kid needs to be seen immediately or not. Sometimes it's obvious from the mother's description that although the child may be coming down with an infection, it's nothing serious, and the best thing to do at that stage is to watch, and wait, and see. But she insists that I can't know what's wrong from the end of the phone and demands a visit. So I crawl out of bed, in a foul mood, to go and examine the kid only to reach the same conclusion I'd come to on the phone.

Situations like the one Dr Taylor described are common enough, and they illustrate the 'experience gap' which exists between doctors and parents. The mother has expectations of how the doctor will determine what is wrong with her child. She extrapolates from her own experience in order to judge what a doctor can, and cannot, reliably diagnose from a description of the baby's condition. Because she could not be certain what was wrong from a description alone, she finds it impossible to believe that a doctor could either.

The GP also finds it difficult to put herself in someone else's shoes; she cannot wipe out all her years of training and experience to become a layman again. Because she can feel confident with a 'telephone diagnosis' she cannot understand the mother's inability to do likewise. Locked inside their different worlds, neither doctor nor parent can bridge the experience gap which separates them.

Most people find it difficult to empathise with anyone whose experience differs materially from their own. Sadly for the world's patients and parents, doctors are no better than anyone else in this respect. I don't intend this as an excuse for doctors

116

not trying; we need to understand why parents think and act as they do, and so must try to recapture memories of our 'pre-doctor' years when we, too, were guided by lay concepts about illness. As a parent you cannot reciprocate such an effort by transforming yourself into a doctor, so you must push for explanations that make a GP's reasoning and advice clear to you. Don't be frightened to ask your doctor questions. If his initial explanations don't make sense to you, tell him why you are still puzzled or concerned. The doctor is no more an expert in communication than you are, and both of you have to make a real effort if you are to communicate effectively with one another. Only by doing this will you have a chance of sharing, and understanding, a doctor's medical perspective.

Since it is an experience gap which sometimes drives a wedge between doctors and parents, the opportunity to care for sick children together – to share a medical experience – can help bring them closer together. Time is a factor they need on their side, for if a family's relationship with their doctor can span several years, many such experiences can be cemented together to build the framework of a successful medical partnership.

Hospital doctors, especially those at a junior level, rarely have the advantage of a long-term relationship with children and their families. When a child is admitted to hospital, the doctors there will probably be strangers to him, so they must get to know the child and family as best they can in a short space of time. Junior doctors working in paediatrics experience the same problems as their peers in other specialties – a heavy workload during the day and arduous rotas at nights and weekends – and these often interfere with their ability to build relationships with children and their parents, as one discontented paediatric SHO at a hospital in Scotland had found:

'A guy who runs in and races out again'

DR ROBBIE KENDALL: I rarely manage to form any sort of relationship with the children or their parents. One of my previous jobs, in paediatric surgery, was an awful lot quieter and I usually managed to become quite good friends with the parents and children. I'd speak to them whenever I saw them, and just have a general chat sometimes, but there's not the opportunity to do that sort of thing here. It's far too busy. I almost never get a chance to play with the children. The only way I'd be able to do that is if I stayed back well after finishing time and you don't often feel like doing that.

GR: Is that dissatisfying for you?

DR ROBBIE KENDALL: Yes. I don't think it's reasonable to have to work at the rate we work at. It isn't pleasing for me or the parents. In Casualty they see me as a guy who runs in, races through a history, examines their kid quickly and races out again, probably after they've waited a couple of hours to be seen.

'The turnover is so quick'

DR BRIDGET JOHNSON, A LIVELY IRISH PAEDIATRIC SHO: I find that the turnover here is so quick that you don't really get the chance to get to know the kids and families. A lot of my patients come in for a batch of tests and then go home two days later, so you don't really build up that much of a relationship with them. It can be different though. I worked in Leicester with kids who had cancer and I was able to spend a lot more time with the parents then, having chats and trying to get things sorted out. I really did enjoy that. I got very close to a lot of the parents and in fact I still keep in contact with some of them.

Despite the pressures of the job, doctors have to find ways of building up a degree of trust with the children admitted to hospital. In order to make a diagnosis and get treatment underway they must somehow transform frightened, screaming babies and toddlers into smiling cherubs who are willing to cooperate. The knack isn't something they teach you at medical school. Dr Jessica Moores, a kindly paediatric SHO in her mid-twenties, working in the north-east Midlands, told me how she dealt with the problem:

'I give the needle a name'

Needles and drips are often the things that frighten kids most. I've used a ploy where I give the needle or the drip a name and they quite like that. When you have to give drugs or fluid through

118

the needle in their vein you say 'Of course Charlie has to have
water and food like anybody else' and they'll usually let you get
on and do it without any fuss. If you can calm them down the
first time round it makes it a lot easier the next time.

Dr Bridget Johnson had also found ways to get round fractious
children:

'I play around a little'

If they're crying and upset there's no point in trying to do anything
unless you can calm them down first. I think that's a knack people
either have or they haven't. I usually give them a toy, chat to
them, play around a little. If it's a baby one of the tricks is to make
sure they've had a feed before you examine them. If they're starving
hungry there's no way you'll be able to do anything. With kids it's
especially difficult examining eyes, ears and throats, but with little
tricks to calm them down you can usually get around the problem.

But how successful are doctors (and nurses for that matter) at
reassuring children and allaying their fears? Some quotes from
children in a book about their experiences in hospital[1] say
clearly what they think:

I think it was very nice in hospital, the nurses are very nice and
they are very playful and the doctors are very kind and gentle . . .
There were lots of other children in the ward I stayed in, it was
nice because the nurses were nice.

If I was a doctor I would invent a new way of giving injections
less painfully.

There's one thing I would like to say and that is, why can't the
doctors and nurses cover up all the knives, scissors, needles etc.?
I think it is mostly these wich [sic] frighten the patients.

As soon as I saw the doctors and nurses I thought they looked
very kind and gentle. And so they were.

I didn't like the doctor because he was ruf [sic].

1. Hales-Tooke, A., *Children in Hospital – The Parents' View*, Priory Press, 1973; pp. 76–8.

Many young doctors find themselves practising paediatrics before they have any offspring of their own, a situation which can create problems both for them and the families they deal with. They may find it hard to understand a parent's natural anxiety and, like some GPs, may too easily label them 'fussing' or 'neurotic'. Dr Bridget Johnson was unmarried when we met, and she described the effort she had to make to empathise with the parents of her young patients:

‘Always listen to the mother’

Sometimes I feel as though I can't possibly have the same insight into a child as the mother has. I've been told by experienced paediatricians to always listen to the mother because no matter how unbelievable whatever she tells you may seem, she'll always be right. And I think it's true. There are times when I've felt, 'Oh for goodness sake, this is ridiculous,' about something a mother says, but it still turns out to be true.

The other thing that's difficult is dealing with parents' anxiety. I think most of them are very anxious when they bring their kids into hospital and sometimes that anxiety can turn to aggression, especially if they're kept waiting in Casualty. If it's a very busy night I'm afraid I do get annoyed. I sometimes feel like saying to them, 'I've only got one pair of hands and I'm working as fast as I can. Your kid certainly isn't as sick as the one in front of him in the queue, so you'll just have to wait.' I'd like to say that but I can't. If you're going to do paediatrics you have to accept that parents get very upset about their kids, but it can be a bit annoying when you're trying to do your best.

Some doctors with no offspring of their own find they have experience of sick children but not healthy ones, and when asked for advice on normal development are embarrassed at their inability to provide a helpful answer. Although, in areas like this, it's inevitable that parents may have more expertise than they do, the inveterate image of doctors as omniscient beings makes it difficult for them to admit their own ignorance:

'I'm not great on children who are well'

DR ROBBIE KENDALL: I think I know quite a bit about sick children, but I'm not that great on children who are well. A mother might say, for example, 'My baby's three and a half months and I was thinking about starting to wean. What do you think about that?' I don't have any children of my own so I have to say that really I've no idea when she should wean her baby.

GR: Do you find it difficult to say 'I don't know' to parents?

DR ROBBIE KENDALL: Yes. I tend to waffle a bit rather than actually say 'I don't know'.

Older, more experienced paediatricians often have children of their own and their ability to relate to young patients and parents is a great help in their work. Sometimes a doctor's own suffering as a parent can help them support others in similarly tragic circumstances as Mr Charles Millington, the paediatric surgeon in Scotland, explained:

'I was on the "other side"'

My twins were born prematurely at 28 weeks and I had to suffer the traumas of a parent sitting watching tiny babies in an incubator. My daughter survived but my son died and I think I learned a lot from that experience. For once I was on the 'other side' – being told incredibly bad news when the babies were six weeks old. I realised afterwards how much I blocked out of what I was told at the time and I think that's why I now give more time to parents whose children are dying, and feel I have more empathy with them.

It was an invaluable experience for me to see things from a parent's point of view. Not all doctors can do that. A colleague of mine was wandering round the special care baby unit one day and saw a father holding the hand of a premature baby in an incubator. I heard him say, 'How can that man sit there all day? It's ridiculous. He can't communicate with the baby,' but he's never said that again after I told him, 'I did that with my baby son.' If it's your own baby it's incredibly important.

Consultants in paediatrics, like those in other specialties, often have more responsibility for out-patients than for ward admissions. The problems referred to the out-patient department are often of a more mundane nature than those appearing as emergency cases on the wards, so a consultant may find himself dealing with rather different childhood complaints from his junior staff. Mr Dougal Cameron, a paediatric surgeon in his sixties, told me with a wry smile about his out-patient work:

'Feet, foreskins and testicles'

Feet, foreskins and testicles – that's what the mothers around here are concerned about, so that's what I see. That and the occasional tummy ache and the odd lump and bump. The practice in out-patients doesn't reflect at all what's up in the ward. Most of the children in out-patients have relatively minor problems so we can book them at four every fifteen minutes and get through them like lightning. Most of the parents come up looking for advice and most of them are prepared to accept what they get. They sometimes find it more difficult to accept advice to do nothing than advice to do something, but that's because they don't understand that the natural history of most things is for self-resolution.

Dr Derek Marshall, a mild-mannered paediatrician at a Scottish teaching hospital, also drew distinctions between the nature of out-patient work and emergency admissions. His clinics ran at a somewhat more leisurely pace than Mr Cameron's:

'Much of what I see is trivial'

Much of what I see in out-patients is fairly trivial stuff. Of course, it may not be trivial to the parents or the patient. They may be very worried about it, and the very fact that they turn up at the hospital and have gone through all the necessary steps to arrive at a consultant's opinion, shows that the problem looms large for them. But medically it may not be anything very much and therefore we can often deal with it on a one-off basis and then send them back to their GP.

Out-patients can become a very pressurised place if you don't watch out. I used to do an awful clinic at an outlying hospital.

On a Wednesday afternoon there would be 12 new patients and 35 follow-ups to be seen, and we started at half-past one and finished at half-past six and then after that you sat and did all the dictating until 9.30 or 10 at night. Fortunately, things are not so hectic at this hospital. I don't usually see more than six patients in a morning and I hope to give them as much time as I feel they need. That's the beauty of the service. I can spend a whole hour with one child, even for quite a small problem. I don't think it's like that in every part of the country. In fact, I'm sure it's not.

Paediatric out-patient services in some hospitals may still leave a lot to be desired, but progress has certainly been made over the last 20 years towards meeting the needs of children and their parents in hospital wards. Pressure from various quarters including NAWCH, the National Association for the Welfare of Children in Hospital, has helped to bring about dramatic changes on paediatric wards. Unrestricted visiting, good facilities for play and education, and provision for relatives who wish to stay overnight have all become much more common, changes which were much appreciated by the parents I spoke to. Janine Dorsey, whose 18-month-old daughter had already been in hospital several times, told me:

'That's much less traumatic'

I'd been in hospital myself as a child and all I can remember about it is bawling non-stop because my mum wasn't there with me. When Becky had her first fit and had to be admitted I was all prepared for a fight in order to stay with her but the staff were wonderful. One of the first things they asked was did I want to sleep at the hospital overnight, and although there wasn't a bed free in the Mothers' Unit, they put up a camp bed beside Becky's cot and let me sleep there. Every time she's been in hospital I've been allowed to wash her, feed her and play with her, just as if she was at home. I think that's made her frequent hospital admissions much less traumatic for both her and me.

Most paediatricians have given wholehearted support to these kind of innovations in hospital care and have also encouraged

123

better communication with children and their families. Such a goal isn't always easy to achieve, as Dr Jessica Moores had discovered:

'Things aren't easy to explain'

You always explain quite fully to the parents what you're doing, why you're doing it, what you expect the outcome will be. You try and take them through what's likely to happen in the next couple of days so that they know what's going on. But you also have to spend time explaining to the kids as well because they can get very frightened if they don't know what's happening. That can take much longer because you've got to put it in children's terms rather than adult terms and sometimes things aren't easy to explain that way.

Communicating with children or parents may be hard for certain young doctors but it is something which experienced paediatricians pride themselves on doing well. They know what a frightening place hospital can be for children and their families, so they make special efforts to minimise the trauma of outpatient visits and ward stays. Mr Dougal Cameron, the Scottish paediatric surgeon, was, despite his stern appearance, a kind-hearted man, concerned to put children at their ease in outpatients.

'You've got to make hospital non-scary'

The children are on unfamiliar territory here. They're not sure what's going to happen to them and they've no idea whether it's going to be pleasant or unpleasant. I think you've got to do as much as you can to make hospital a non-scary experience for them. Sometimes you can't avoid it being scary – they're frightened by X-ray machines, needles and all sorts of other things, but you've got to do as much as you can to make sure they won't be frightened to come back and see you the next time. For that reason I usually don't draw blood from them. If it's necessary I'll ask one of the phlebotomists to do it, partly because they're better at doing it, and partly because it's me the child has to come and see again and that way I hope they won't associate me with the wicked folk who stick needles in them.

'We have to keep them informed'

DR DEREK MARSHALL: I try and speak to all the parents who have a child admitted to my ward. My juniors will have spoken to them too. We all have a responsibility to keep the child and the parents informed as to what's happening and what we're thinking. I believe that's something that is well done in paediatrics and is not well done in adult medicine. Adult wards have set visiting hours during which doctors make themselves scarce. They should be more like paediatric wards – open visiting hours with doctors making a point of speaking to relatives.

From my talks with numerous paediatricians it was clear they felt that communication was one of their strong points and I wondered if parents and nursing staff agreed. The mothers I spoke to on paediatric wards in several hospitals certainly seemed pleased with the accessibility of doctors and their willingness to discuss any queries or worries they voiced. This comment from the mother of a two-year-old girl in a Midlands hospital was typical of the remarks I heard:

'The doctors have been great'

The doctors have been great. If I had any worries I just said to the nurse, 'Could I have a word with the doctor?' and they'd come along and chat about it and put my mind at ease as best they could.

The sample of parents I interviewed was very small and more extensive surveys assessing consumer views of paediatric services have revealed that not all parents are as pleased as those I spoke to. Bolton Community Health Council, for example, produced a report [2] in 1985 based on the results of questionnaires completed by parents of 74 children who had been in-patients at local hospitals. Although the report commented that 'the level of satisfaction with services was very high overall' it also said that 'communication was the largest single ground for complaint'. Communication problems with staff had played a

2. 'Children's Hospital Services Survey' by Bolton Community Health Council, December 1985.

large part in some parents' dissatisfaction with admission and discharge procedures, general care on the wards, visiting arrangements and facilities for relatives. I asked Anna White, a nursing sister on one of the paediatric wards I visited, if she thought poor communication caused problems for children and their parents:

'Problems aren't always the fault of doctors'

From my experience in paediatrics I'd say poor communication is less of a problem in this specialty than in many others. A lot of our medical staff have children themselves, especially the more senior ones, and I think they're able to be far more appreciative of what parents go through. Unfortunately, doctors don't always appreciate parents' anxieties. They'll walk in, say something, and then walk out, and they won't realise the implication for the parent, especially if they use medical terminology carelessly. I've heard a doctor examining a baby say, 'Oh yes, I can feel a pyloric tumour,' and as soon as the doctor had gone the mother started having hysterics because to her the word tumour meant a death sentence on her child. I had to go back and explain that 'tumour' is simply medical terminology for a lump and that in her child's case it wasn't anything to do with cancer.

Communication problems aren't always the fault of doctors and nurses. Sure, we do sometimes forget to give parents information, or give information in a way they can't understand, but there may be other reasons why parents say they haven't been told anything. I know myself that I've sat and talked to people in simple layman's language, explaining things, and the next day they've said to a staff nurse that no one's told them anything so she's explained again, and later the same day they've come back to me saying, 'What's going on? Nobody's told us.' The problem is their anxiety. I think they feel that if they hear things said several times they'll understand them.

So if you're the parent of a sick child and you feel dissatisfied with the information provided by doctors or nurses, what can you do to improve the situation? Firstly, you need to identify what's given rise to the communication problem. Is it that the staff simply haven't been available to speak to you? Or is it that they've tried to give you information, but you found this difficult to take in, understand or believe? If it's mainly that you haven't been given sufficient opportunities to question the staff, then ask if the nurse in charge of the ward can speak to you, perhaps at a prearranged time if she's busy when you first voice your request. Similarly, don't rely on trying to catch a doctor when he comes on the ward, but ask the ward sister if she can arrange a specific time for you to talk with him. Both doctors and nurses are more likely to devote their attention to you and your concerns if they have set aside time for the meeting rather than being collared when they're busy attending to other tasks.

If you've spoken to staff and still feel confused or anxious, think about the questions you have which still remain un-answered. Write them down if there's a chance you might forget them; consider taking someone else with you when you meet the doctor or nurse – afterwards they may be able to remember important points you have forgotten; and if terms or explanations are used which you don't understand, don't be afraid to say so. Doctors and nurses constantly need reminding *not* to use medical jargon which merely confuses and mystifies other people.

Parents' intense anxiety about their sick child may contribute to communication problems at times, but it is wholly understand-able. Equally intelligible is the distress of parents whose child is dying. Few doctors could fail to appreciate their suffering, so caring for these children and their families can be very stressful. Dr Jessica Moores had needed to tell several couples that their sick baby was unlikely to recover and she described the agony of doing so:

‘Their distress inevitably affects you’

It's never easy because each time you're dealing with a different set of people and obviously babies and kids are particularly precious. It's not the same as telling someone that their 80-year-old relative is going to pass away – it's far more emotional. To find the right words for that particular set of people is always very difficult and although you can give them a little bit of hope you can't give them much in the way of reassurance in case you

127

build their hopes too high. I think their distress inevitably affects you. You have to learn to let it out when you get home, either by talking or by crying if that's more appropriate.

Dr Dick Hamilton, a consultant paediatrician in northern England, told me how years of experience had helped him respond appropriately to bereaved parents and how, occasionally, it was parents who showed him new ways of coping with a child's death.

'I thought there was a party on'

It's certainly got much easier the longer I've been doing it. Any child dying is still traumatic – I still feel as uptight about it inside, but I think I can outwardly cope with it better and so help parents more. With families that don't know me I try my best not to become emotional. I don't think it would help them if I burst into tears, so I try to stay quite calm. But if I know the family well we'll have a good cry together and I don't feel bad about that. With them, I don't think I need to hide the fact that I'm upset.

One of my patients, an 18-month-old baby called Emily, died at home a while ago and because her parents knew that she was going to die they'd given it an awful lot of thought and had worked out exactly what they were going to do. I went round to their house that night and as I drove into the cul-de-sac where they lived I thought there was a party on. Everyone's doors were open and people were going backwards and forwards from the house. As I walked through the front door I saw 15 to 20 people downstairs, all chatting and drinking coffee, and upstairs I found the parents sitting on a bed with Emily in her cot, laid out very nicely. We sat there for an hour and a half just chatting; people came in and picked up Emily and cuddled her, and the parents and I sat and gave her a cuddle too. The atmosphere in that house was amazing. I wasn't expecting anything like that and when I walked out of there I thought, I don't believe this. It may sound awful to say it, but it was a very pleasant experience, totally new for me. I mean there's no way I would have thought of handling it that way but it was brilliant and the parents have been absolutely fine ever since.

Of course not every family copes with the death of a child as successfully as Emily's parents did. Brian Patterson and his wife lost their four-month-old baby as a cot death and both of them found it impossible to come to terms with what had happened.

'There was terrible guilt'

Perhaps it was because there was no warning that Katy was ill that made it so difficult for us to accept that she'd died. One day she was there, apparently happy and well, and the next morning we found her dead in her cot. Everyone from the ambulance men to the nurses and doctors were very kind, but no one could give us any answers as to why it had happened. Even the post-mortem didn't give us any clues. I think we both felt cheated and angry, as well as distraught, that our daughter had been taken away from us. And guilty too. There was a terrible burden of guilt, wondering if there was something we'd done, or maybe failed to do, that had caused her death. For at least a year afterwards my wife and I both retreated into ourselves, unable to talk about it, or to support one another. Our marriage nearly fell apart and it's only now, two years after Katy died, that we're beginning to emerge from the depression and despair.

For Dr Hamilton and most other paediatricians, the deaths they have to cope with are relatively few when compared with the large numbers of children they treat successfully and restore to health. A few doctors specialise in the care of childhood leukaemia and cancer and, as a result, have to deal with many more dying children and bereaved families. One, a friendly, loquacious man who spoke with great candour, told me about the very stressful nature of this work:

'It's just too much'

DR BOB AYERS: We have a whole series of people we're very fond of, and very close to, dying, and that's very hard. Of course it's hardest for the patient, but it's also hard for the family and very hard for the staff and it produces a lot of tensions. It's the continuous nature of the work that makes it so hard. One or two of my colleagues in this field have had quite serious emotional breakdowns and I can see why. It's just too much.

GR: Do you talk much together about the stress you're experiencing or is it more the case that nobody talks about it until someone cracks?

DR BOB AYERS: I think that's right. Generally, in medicine, doctors don't talk about emotional things. And when a colleague has a problem they don't want to know. My colleagues here, nice as many of them are, really don't want to know. I find it a big dilemma. I mean I get my support from within the family, from my wife, and every so often we have a big barney because the work can take over and your family suffer, there's no doubt about it. My family have suffered quite badly at times and I know that. I think that's one of the dilemmas: you want to get away and have a life outside work but every parent sees the care of their sick child as *your* responsibility. It becomes a vicious circle and you do get to the point of saying, 'I just can't cope.' I've been in that situation for the last two to three months and I haven't found support from my medical colleagues. One colleague, who is actually quite understanding of the problem, won't let it intrude. He doesn't wish to step over from being a professional colleague to being a personal friend, so he tends to be flippant and say, 'Come off it, don't blame your patients.' I think the problem in medicine is that people will take everything that you offer and go on taking until you draw the limits. And you have to draw limits because otherwise you'll burn out. I think burn-out is a problem after ten years in this field. My colleagues around the country don't believe that. Well, some of them talk about it, but they won't admit to it.

The stress of paediatric oncology is self-evident, but the work provides much joy too, as Dr Christine Donaldson pointed out:

'It isn't all doom and gloom'

It isn't all doom and gloom in paediatric oncology. Plenty of nice things happen too. All these photos above my desk are of children who survived their leukaemia and are off treatment now.
[Pointing to a photograph of a smiling teenager in army uniform.] This fellow's granny brought me this picture. He was treated when he was two and now he's 18 and passed out from the Fusiliers which is terrific. I find that very rewarding.

The rewards of working with children (and not only those

who recover from potentially fatal illnesses) were made clear by many of the paediatricians I interviewed. Parents' gratitude for the care they deliver boosts their job satisfaction, and for many doctors there are bonuses in having children, rather than adults, as patients.

Mr Charles Millington: Dealing with children brings everything very much down to earth. It's different from other specialties because you don't just have a relationship with your patient but with the parents as well. That's part of the challenge.

Dr Bob Ayers: I don't like formality. I tend to work in shirtsleeves and never wear a white coat in front of the kids. I guess it's the nature of kids that means you can't, or shouldn't, be too pompous in paediatrics. I think that kids deflate you. You have to be more relaxed when you're dealing with children. So I like it when the kids say I'm daft. I think that's a kind of compliment from them.

'Who else would tell an entire audience they'd been circumcised?'

Dr Dick Hamilton: Paediatrics is incredibly rewarding. It's very nice to be told every day, and we *are* told every day, what brilliant people we are. To be honest, Mother Nature does most of it for us, but it really is very nice to be told over and over again what a good job you're doing.

I suppose another reason I like paediatrics is because children are so honest. Something that happened only about two weeks ago brought that home to me. I'd gone to a local primary school to receive a cheque from the Parent-Teacher Association because they'd raised some money for the paediatric unit. The whole school was assembled: all the kids, sitting down, looking pristine, all the teachers down the side of the hall and lots of parents at the back. The PTA lady handed me the cheque and asked if I'd like to say a few words. So I got down on my haunches to talk to the kids first and I said, 'I'm a children's doctor at the Infirmary. Who know's the Infirmary?' And all these little hands shot up – 'Sir!' 'Sir!' 'Sir!' So we had a banter and I explained what we were going to do with the money and then I said, 'Who was it said they knew the Infirmary?' All the hands went up again and there was a little boy, a few rows down, straining to be seen, obviously desperate for me to ask him a question. So I said to

131

him, 'What were you in with?' and straight away, at the top of his voice, he said, 'They chopped the end of me willy off, sir!' and the whole place erupted! Kids are so truthful. I mean, who else, other than a six-year-old, would stand up and tell an entire audience they'd been circumcised?

Caring for sick children obviously provides doctors with a mixture of difficulty and delight, sorrow and celebration. Despite the technical, practical and emotional difficulties of administering medical care to children, many of the doctors I spoke to felt they were the most endearing patients one could ask for. Paediatricians seem to me to be some of the most satisfied of all doctors; it therefore came as no surprise when I asked Dr Hamilton if there was anything about his work he didn't like and he replied with a broad smile, 'No, I've got the best job in the world.'

CHAPTER 7

ACUTE ILLNESS

AN ACUTE ILLNESS – one of sudden onset, relatively short duration and with severe symptoms – may catapult a patient into contact with doctors when they least expect it. Anything from a bad dose of flu to life-threatening hepatitis may necessitate a doctor's help, and for people who are usually healthy such an episode may be one of the few occasions when they deal with doctors and see inside the medical world. Exactly who those doctors are is dictated, to some extent, by the nature and severity of the illness, for certain problems can be managed by a GP alone while others require urgent admission to hospital. The role each doctor plays likewise depends on where medical management takes place and all these factors influence the way doctor and patient relate to one another.

Most people consult their GP when an acute illness lays them low. Some conditions are self-limiting, like gastroenteritis and chickenpox; no treatment as such is necessary, so the GP's main role is to provide reassurance and medication to ease unpleasant symptoms while the body itself tackles the infection. Minor illnesses such as tonsillitis, bronchitis or a urine infection are usually straightforward to diagnose and treat; after one or two visits the patient will probably have no further need to see the doctor.

With a more serious medical problem the GP has, in addition to making his diagnosis, to decide where best the patient can be treated. The choice between hospital and home is not always as simple as it might seem. Numerous factors have to be taken into consideration: for example, the nature of investigations to be carried out and the type of treatment needed, the nursing care required, the patient's own wishes and his social circumstances, including the ability of any family to cope with him at home. In addition, the GP must consider the availability of specific community services that the patient might need, and decide whether he himself has the time, confidence and willingness to take sole responsibility for managing the illness.

A doctor's training teaches him the skills of detective work. He gathers clues from the patient's story of the illness and from carrying out a physical examination, then pieces together the information to create a jigsaw puzzle picture of the diagnosis. Nowadays, the doctor can also order any number of investigations to confirm his diagnosis or provide more detailed information if he is still uncertain about the exact nature of the illness. Sometimes it seems as if the doctor's own clinical skills have been superseded by medical technology, for the results of blood tests, X-rays and other investigations will build up a far more detailed picture of the problem than the doctor can using his eyes, ears and hands alone.

In an emergency situation, however, a GP must rely solely on his own diagnostic skills to work out what is wrong. With a seriously ill patient, the doctor must make a rapid assessment of the problem and take swift action to ensure that the correct treatment is administered without delay. It is undoubtedly a nerve-wracking time for the GP, but one which many find an exciting challenge. It can be rewarding too, if the doctor 'gets it right' and saves the patient from a potentially life-threatening illness.

The doctor's own personality has a considerable bearing on his attitude to acute medicine. Dr Stephen Kerr, the 'practical, DIY' GP obstetrician enjoyed this area of his work a great deal:

'It's very "hot"'

I enjoy trying to make the diagnosis in an acute illness. If you get a good, interesting case once a week it gives you a lot of satisfaction and you can put up with the more mundane stuff. I enjoy managing acute problems more than long-term chronic illness, but that's my personality I think. I suppose that's one of the attractions of the obstetrics. It's very 'hot' for 24 hours or so and then it's virtually over and done with.

The more reflective and analytical GP, Dr Tom Peterson, had become increasingly interested in the psychological aspects of illness during his 20-odd years in general practice, and so had a rather different view of acute medicine:

'What is interesting is the person not the appendix'

I now find the physical, scientific end of medicine less interesting. I think when you've seen appendicitis a hundred times you have seen appendicitis, as such. What then becomes interesting is the person around the appendix, not the appendix. I do enjoy acute medicine in the sense that one can get something 'right', but sometimes that's tempered by the knowledge that having got it right, it might be very bad news for the patient.

Called to the scene of an emergency, the GP has little time to sit and ponder over the best course of action. He must make his decision quickly, for as time ticks by the patient's condition may worsen. With certain medical problems management decisions are difficult, because views on the 'correct' treatment have changed over the years and go on changing, leaving the GP with no absolute guidelines on what to do. A coronary, or heart attack, is one of the conditions which can present the GP with this kind of a dilemma.

'Whatever you do, you've got to do quickly'

DR ANGELA LEIGH: My heart always sinks when there's a call that could be a coronary because there's a whole lot of stresses associated with coronaries. It's out of the blue very often, it's comparatively young people who are affected, and there's been such a changing attitude to treatment over the years. We've gone through various phases of active treatment on the part of the GP. In the early seventies we were giving one treatment for some cases and another treatment for others and really it was a great strain because you're in a stressful situation and whatever you've got to do, you've got to do quickly, and to decide between various options was difficult, and you'd wonder at the end of the day if you'd done the wrong thing. It then became a bit more simplified and the main advice was to control pain which is a

135

relatively easy thing to do, but I think I still carry within me the sort of stress there was in the seventies.

Also, in our practice there's always been a policy to treat the majority of coronaries at home, so that's time consuming because you're going to have to make a lot of visits, two or three in the first day and so on, and then you're always at risk, if the patient does die, of the relatives saying, 'Shouldn't you have sent him into hospital?' I think I now find the stress of coronaries more difficult to handle than I did, say, ten years ago. It's more of a strain now that I'm older.

For many acute conditions there is little debate over the best form of treatment, but the GP must still decide whether he has the skill to administer the treatment successfully.

'There are areas where I can cope and areas where I can't'

DR TOM PETERSON: Whether or not I manage an acute problem at home partly depends on the skills needed. There are certain areas of technical expertise where I know I can cope and certain areas where I know I can't. If I'm confronted with a child with asthma, for example, I usually think I can quite reasonably deal with it by using a nebuliser [1] because this is an expertise that I have and that I feel confident in. But there are other conditions that I would prefer to share with a specialist because I think the doctor who carries on alone is exposed to an extent, and there are limits to which any doctor should expose themselves in isolated activity.

Dr Peterson also pointed out the need to consider the patient's expectations when deciding on how to manage the illness:

I think you must endeavour to perceive the patient's expectations of you. They may well think that asthma is something a GP might manage on his own and that glandular fever is something that almost certainly he *will* manage on his own. But if the problem involved something like cancer I think they would have the feeling that this wasn't something that the general practitioner

1. An apparatus for converting liquid medications into fine spray. By breathing in the spray, an asthmatic patient will usually get relief from their symptoms.

136

handled alone, and you need to take note of their expectations in deciding how to manage the problem.

If the GP does decide to admit the patient to hospital he may then find that his problems are far from over. There are often precious few beds available for emergency cases and the GP may have to reason, bargain or plead with the hospital doctor in charge of acute admissions to find room for his patient. I can remember one nerve-wracking occasion when this happened to me. I had been called to a patient's flat because her 30-year-old son was in 'a very distressed state'. When I arrived I found that the man was obviously mentally ill and needed to be admitted to hospital for his own safety and that of his mother. He was shouting abuse at her, and threatening to kill both of them. He resented the fact that a doctor had been called and so began to threaten me too.

After nearly an hour of cajoling, the man agreed to be admitted but he continued to hurl loud abuse at me as I nervously telephoned the hospital. The doctor I spoke to seemed unmoved by the screaming and shouting which were clearly audible as I explained the dangerous situation I was dealing with, and at first he refused to admit the man, suggesting instead that I contact another hospital, some 20 miles away, where he had been a patient several years before. In the end it was only my whispered pleading, and the man's attempts to smash the telephone as I held it, which convinced the doctor that the patient needed to be admitted to his hospital without delay. Fifteen minutes later I breathed a sigh of relief when an ambulance arrived, with a police escort, to accompany the man to hospital.

Sometimes the GP is not even given the chance to put his case in person to the hospital doctor controlling admissions. Some areas employ an emergency bed service or 'bed bureau' to allocate acute admissions to hospitals in the region, according to their available bed space. The GP cannot then discuss the case with a hospital colleague or choose where the patient will be admitted; the matter becomes something of a lottery and both GP and patient have to accept whatever they're offered. Dr Angela Leigh found it a trying problem to deal with:

'You don't know where they'll end up'

Very rarely now can you admit to the district general hospital directly. You have to go to the bed bureau instead. I loathe that because I like to be able to talk to the registrar who's going to see the patient. You put as much information as you can in the letter that you send with them but you can't put down absolutely everything, so it's much better to talk to someone about them. And you don't know where they're going to end up. It could be any of the hospitals around here. The bed situation for certain specialties is very bad, so for some acute problems, like a stroke, I don't even attempt to get them into hospital unless they live alone or have a very elderly spouse who couldn't possibly look after them.

A recent report by the group Birmingham Consultants for Rescue of the NHS[2] highlighted the fact that some patients are dying because their GPs find it so difficult to arrange their admission to hospital. Between September 1988 and February 1989, the group received 52 complaints from GPs about difficulty in admitting acutely ill patients to local hospitals. The alarming cases reported included:

- a 51-year-old woman with a suspected heart attack who died during the 45 minutes it took to arrange an admission.

- an 80-year-old patient with a fractured leg for whom the GP spent an hour and a half contacting six different hospitals before managing to arrange admission at three a.m.

- a woman who had been seen as an out-patient on the previous day but was refused admission because her local hospital was on 'red alert'. She was finally admitted to another hospital where her complicated medical history was not known.

- a 65-year-old man with a suspected heart attack whose GP was told that the hospital was accepting 999 calls only so he had to use that system to have the man admitted.

2. 'Counting the Cost of Cost-Cutting', Birmingham Consultants for Rescue of the NHS, March 1989.

Even if the GP does manage to find a hospital bed for his patient, he may then find it difficult to keep tabs on their treatment and progress. Communication problems are a notorious bone of contention between doctors in hospitals and general practice, with each camp blaming the other for their faults. Hospital staff accuse GPs of being difficult to get hold of, and we are! Many of our duties – home visits, meetings, case conferences etc. – take us out of our surgeries so we can't be reached immediately when colleagues want us. On the other hand, hospital doctors often don't appreciate that it is GPs who resume responsibility for patients' medical care when they leave hospital, and their frequent failure to relay information to us before, or soon after, the patient's discharge can result in serious problems.

'I'm sent a scappy bit of paper'

DR HILARY TAYLOR: It makes me mad sometimes when a patient comes out of hospital and I'm sent a scrappy bit of paper from the houseman with just a list of drugs that the patient went home on. No diagnosis, nothing. So I have to play a guessing game, trying to work out what the problem was that they were admitted for. Often it's perfectly simple to deduce what the problem was but occasionally it's not, and both the patient and I get confused about what needs doing once they've been discharged because neither of us have had any detailed information from the hospital. If I try to phone the doctor concerned to get more information the hospital lines are usually engaged, or the doctor doesn't answer his bleep, or if I *do* manage to get in touch with him he can't remember the patient and the specific details I need.

I can understand why it happens. When I was a houseman and SHO I was too busy with all my other duties to write proper discharge letters, and because I'd never been a GP I didn't realise how important that letter could be. As far as I was concerned, when the patient left hospital that was the end of my responsibility for them.

Some of the communication problems between hospital doctors and GPs arise because the hospital all too easily becomes a little world of its own, divorced from the rest of life 'outside'. Everything in hospital revolves around medicine; everyone's attention is focused on disease, investigation, treatment and cure. To hospital doctors an acute illness has a kind of completeness about it: they can date its onset, monitor its lifespan and watch its extinction as treatment begins to work. The average acute stay has a neat beginning, middle and end, and it is all too easy for doctors to forget that the patient has a life before and after hospital.

This separation of hospital from the rest of life doesn't only affect the hospital doctor's efforts to communicate with GPs. It also has a profound influence on the way they relate to patients. The regulation uniform of pyjamas, dressing gown and slippers helps to make a patient anonymous in hospital, so that their life and personality retreat into insignificance while their illness becomes the centre of attention. This doesn't mean that all hospital doctors see their patients as just 'the stroke in bed six' or 'the gall bladder in bed four', but for many it is a struggle to direct their efforts towards anything other than physical problems because both their medical training and their experience on over-burdened hospital wards emphasise this as the main objective of hospital treatment.

In theory at least, housemen spend more time with acutely ill patients than senior hospital doctors because it is their job to see to the day-to-day running of the wards. Unfortunately, the workload they have to contend with often means that they spend only a minor part of the day actually talking with patients. Dr Simon McCarthy, a houseman in a Cheltenham hospital, described the end result of his busy schedule:

'I lose sight of the patients'

I notice that when I get very hurried, when I've got hundreds of things to do, and some very pleasant patient is trying to have a conversation with me, I just want to say, 'Stop!' I'm in the horns of a dilemma: I'd quite like to talk with them, but then again I've got all these things to do and they have to be done. Sometimes I think I actually lose sight of the patients because of all the other things I have to do.

Many housemen find they never get to know much more about their patients than the medical problem that brought them into hospital.

Some housemen, like Dr Graham Hunt, prefer this kind of detached relationship with patients, and shy away from any greater involvement with them.

'I stand back a little bit'

I try not to get involved with patients too much. It's a conscious decision. I try and stand back a little bit.

I never really thought I would have to get involved with the patients because in hospital I don't have to look after them for very long, hopefully. They come and go. I just clerk them in, talk to them a bit then, and see them on ward rounds. It's a bit like a conveyor belt.

Other housemen I spoke to found their detachment from patients more of a worry. They realised that seeing people away from their home environment, and during a short stay in hospital only, made it difficult to relate to them in the way they would like to.

'It's only when they die that you meet their relatives'

DR LISA WESTBURY, THE HOUSEMAN WORKING IN THE NORTH-EAST MIDLANDS: I've been slightly distressed sometimes at how I see my patients. It's a bit intangible really but it's something that's shocked me. I do see them as 'patients' and not as 'people' sometimes.

It's only when they die that you meet their relatives and realise that they really were people with a home and a whole family network you never knew anything about. That's something general practice would bring – you see people so much more in their own setting, whereas in hospital I see them on a trolley in Casualty and to me they're a patient who either needs a drip put up or a blood sample taken.

Dr Hassan Khan, born in India but resident in the UK for most of his life, also regretted not knowing his patients better:

141

'You just haven't got the time'

It would be nice to get to know patients more completely because it would prevent some of the rather unfortunate accidents when, without being aware of it, you send somebody home to a really appalling social problem which you haven't had time to look into, or haven't been interested in. It would also be nice, in a purely personal sense, if you knew the patients that much better. I do sometimes feel a little bit bad when you know a patient's dying to have a long talk and you just haven't got the time. Or sometimes it's not even time, it's just the energy and motivation. You feel so tired that you think, I've got better things to do.

As with any relationship, one between a doctor and patient takes time to develop. With increasing pressure on hospital services, patients tend to be sent home much sooner than in the past and so are often on the ward for only a few days. Not surprisingly, when the turnover rate of patients is high, doctors are less able, and perhaps also less willing, to spend time getting to know people who will be discharged after only a few days, and whom they will probably never see again.

Nowadays a longer hospital stay usually implies a more serious problem, and while this is obviously worrying for the patient and their family, it does give them more of a chance to get to meet and talk with the medical staff, which can itself be important in recovery.

Junior doctors often find the extra time a bonus too, as Dr Tessa Collins described:

The hospital has a blanket policy that patients have to be kept in for ten days if they've had a definite M.I.[3] and longer if they develop complications. I find that you definitely build up more of a relationship with them than with other patients because they're in for longer.

Housemen rarely have the opportunity to follow up the patients they see on the ward because medical care is usually continued either by the GP or by more senior hospital doctors in the out-patient clinic to which the patient returns some weeks

3. M.I. is the abbreviation for myocardial infarction, the medical term for a heart attack.

later. The few housemen who do take part in follow-up clinics seem to find it helpful in motivating them to take an interest in more than just the patient's illness. Knowing that they will see a patient again, sometime after they've been discharged from hospital, helps the junior doctor to relate the hospital admission to the rest of the patient's life and to recognise that it is a person they're treating, not just a medical problem.

'It's nice to see people when they're well'

DR HELEN BADCOCK, THE HOUSEMAN AT A SMALL HOSPITAL IN KENT: At this hospital we do regular clinics once or twice a week where we see all the old in-patients. Everyone who's been discharged comes and sees the houseman first, which I think's an excellent idea. Around here there's a fairly middle-class population, and there are some elderly gentlemen who turn up to the clinic looking really smart in their three-piece suits with a carnation in their buttonhole. They look so different from when they were on the ward in a pair of hospital pyjamas, that sometimes you barely recognise them! It's nice to see people when they're well and back to ordinary life. It's very satisfying.

Emergency episodes sometimes produce the kind of drama that fuels medical soaps and perpetuates the heroic Dr Kildare image of the hospital doctor.

Perhaps the most vivid example is the scenario in which a patient suffers a cardiac arrest. They may well be saved by a doctor's skill but medical help must arrive within minutes if there is to be any hope of survival. In hospital there is always a 'crash team' on alert to deal with such an emergency. The team usually consists of the junior doctors on take that day, as well as a designated nurse and anaesthetist, all of whom carry special bleeps with which they can be summoned if needed. When a cardiac arrest call goes out, all hell breaks loose: nurses fly to the patient's side and hurriedly draw screens around them, while the crash team arrives at full pelt, white coat-tails flapping behind them, quickly converging over the unconscious body. Meanwhile, porters rush vital resuscitation equipment to the scene and a desperate attempt to revive the patient begins.

143

It is easy for such a dramatic event to be glamorised in a book or television series, but what does it really feel like to be a doctor summoned by a crash call? Housemen are usually scared out of their wits. They hover anxiously on the edge of the scene uncertain what to do, or wade in, trembling, in a vain attempt to be useful. Dr Tessa Collins was one of several housemen who told me they dreaded their crash bleep going off:

'I feel physically sick'

I don't think there's anything glamorous about cardiac arrest calls at all. I hate them, really can't bear them. If the arrest bleep goes off when I'm asleep and I have to leap out of bed and run up three or four floors to get to the ward I feel physically sick when I get there. I feel really good if we manage to bring somebody round, but then again I feel really awful if we don't. There was a spell recently when we had a run of people who'd collapsed and we hadn't been able to resuscitate and I got really depressed about that. One of them was a fairly young chap. We were waiting for him to arrive in Casualty in the middle of the night because we'd heard he was in a really bad state. We pulled him out of the ambulance and started trying to resuscitate him but it was a real no-hoper. It shook me that the man was young and yet we hadn't been able to do anything to save him. A nurse who was there started preaching at us telling us what we should be doing and afterwards said 'That man could've been my husband', blaming us for not pulling him through. That was very distressing.

SHOs and registrars usually cope better with emergencies like cardiac arrest calls because they have more experience, and therefore more confidence, in how to handle the necessary practical procedures. They also become more realistic about the likely outcome. After my first couple of years on the wards I realised that although I still hoped people would survive a cardiac arrest, I no longer expected them to, so I wasn't plagued with the distress and guilt that I'd felt as a new houseman when our attempts at resuscitation failed. I undoubtedly became hardened to this kind of sudden death, particularly in patients I didn't know, and while that gave me some cause for concern, it was certainly helpful during the emergency itself when only a calm, detached and logical mind can ensure that procedures are carried out swiftly and correctly.

Such detachment may not be complete; I would find myself wondering momentarily who the dying person was, what he'd done with his life, and how his family would cope if he died. Gazing at the pair of vacant eyes with their rapidly dilating pupils, I was often reminded that as a doctor I'm one of the few people nowadays who witness death occurring. As I watched patients slip away I wondered what they were aware of while we pushed oxygen into their lungs and drugs into their veins in an effort to keep them alive. No amount of physiological knowledge could answer this question for me, and after several more years in medicine during which I have seen many more people die, I think death is a process as mysterious and marvellous as birth.

As doctors rise through the hospital ranks, most become less and less involved with the acute end of medicine. Consultant surgeons and anaesthetists are sometimes called in to help with emergencies but in most specialties the acute problems are dealt with by junior staff. Although consultants are usually on call as often as their juniors, they don't have to be resident in the hospital while on duty. Sometimes they'll be telephoned at home for advice, but they rarely have to leave their beds if there is an experienced registrar or senior registrar on call in the hospital. Not surprisingly, consultants are glad to be relieved of nights of broken sleep, and most consider this ample compensation for the loss of involvement in exciting emergency work.

'To some extent I miss it'

DR DEREK MARSHALL, THE CONSULTANT PAEDIATRICIAN AT A TEACHING HOSPITAL IN SCOTLAND: To some extent I miss not being primarily involved in the wards, but I don't think I could maintain that involvement and do all the other things I have to do as well. It's probably better that patients are seen by juniors because, as time goes by, most consultants in my sort of post are less able to deal with the acute crises of a Casualty

145

department than they were. You become less familiar with it on a
day-to-day basis, and less technically adept as your role changes
over the years.

'I would find it difficult to do that now'

DR MALCOLM WHITTINGTON, THE WEST-COUNTRY OBSTETRICIAN:
Being at deliveries is an enjoyable part of obstetrics because it's
nearly always a happy occasion, but on the other hand you
have to be out of bed during the night and although as a registrar
I had to work all day and all night and all the next day too, I
would find it very difficult to do that now. I do a bit – assisting
with deliveries for colleagues' wives and the occasional private
patient – which keeps the skills going and gives me some
satisfaction, but I wouldn't like the kind of job where it was just
me on with a junior SHO so I'd have to be up all night whenever
I was on call.

As I've mentioned earlier, consultants tend to accept their
role as overseers of care in acute cases. They have to let their
juniors gain experience by managing the acute admissions
largely on their own, whilst at the same time ensuring that no
mistakes are made or problems missed. Dr Alan Morris, a 37-
year-old consultant in the north-east Midlands, described his
involvement with acutely ill patients on his wards:

'I make a point of seeing them'

I think it's terribly important that I make a point of seeing them,
even if it's just to say 'Hello, my name's Dr Morris' and shake
them by the hand. Whether it does any good or not I don't
know, but I feel they should have the sense that even if I've not
personally examined them, and in the majority I haven't, I have at
least been aware of the circumstances that have led up to their
admission, why they're in, and what's been done. Then they just
hear my conclusion that the way things are going is the way
things should be going, and I try and give them some idea of
how long they're likely to be in hospital. Doctors often spend a
lot of time writing pages of admission notes and sending off lots
of tests, but what we don't spend much time doing is sending
people out. I think that side of things is often forgotten by the

nursing staff and junior doctors, so much of what I do on a ward round is aimed towards making things happen after they leave hospital rather than taking care of what's happening while they're in it.

'I don't breathe down the neck of my registrar'

DR MICHAEL HILLIER, THE CONSULTANT IN GENERAL AND RENAL MEDICINE FROM A NORTH WALES DISTRICT GENERAL HOSPITAL: My juniors admit the acute cases and what I'm providing is a modulation for the patient. I'm trying to maintain and improve the standards of the junior staff. I don't want to breathe down the neck of my registrar too excessively. I want to give him a certain amount of rope, but on the other hand I do need to keep a fairly close watch on what's going on. In a sense I'm awarding marks for the patient's management and making sure that no large-sized clangers have been dropped because people didn't stop and think about something.

This 'supervisor' role which most consultants adopt for acutely ill patients explains why some people never even meet 'the boss', let alone get to know him, during their short stay in hospital. Discussions often take place away from the bedside amongst the team of doctors and if a medical problem has responded well to treatment the consultant may agree to the patient's discharge without actually seeing him. Routine ward rounds give the consultant an opportunity to meet his patients but they are often just as much a vehicle for emptying beds as for making acquaintance with the current occupants. Mr Dougal Cameron, the Scottish paediatric surgeon, summed up the situation he often faced on his team's 'take' or 'waiting' day:

'Who can you get rid of?'

You've got to start your waiting day with enough beds to cope with your anticipated load. Very often the first round of the morning is concerned not so much with how the patients are but who you can get rid of. That always happens when you've got a commitment to both emergency and elective care in the same unit.

147

With the ever-present problem of hospital bed shortages, consultants may have to be ruthless in making decisions about which patients can stay and which must be discharged to make room for the emergency admissions on the team's next 'take' day. No seriously ill patient would ever be sent home purely to create more bed space, but those who are convalescing may well have to be discharged to the care of family, GP and community nurses when ideally they should be allowed to stay in hospital a little longer.

For some patients their stay in hospital is so brief that they hardly have time to come to terms with their illness and admission before they are on their way home again. Many will have little contact with the doctors involved in their care: the GP's visit seems to be over in a flash and, once in hospital, the patient may see the juniors only fleetingly each day and the consultant on his bi-weekly ward rounds. So what can be done if you, the patient, or your relatives feel dissatisfied with this kind of medical management? If you have questions about your illness or its treatment, don't forget that the nurses may be able to provide the answers, so do try asking them. If there are matters you specifically want to discuss with a doctor then voice them to him at the first opportunity. If he seems too busy to answer your queries satisfactorily there and then, ask if he can suggest a more convenient time when you could talk to him at greater length.

If you feel that you or your family won't be able to cope when you're discharged from hospital, talk to the ward sister or doctor about sources of help that could be provided at home. Physiotherapy, district nurse visits, a Home Help and Meals on Wheels are just some of the services which it may be possible to organise for you, making an early discharge from hospital less daunting. Remember, too, that it is a GP's role to continue caring for you once you are back home, and that the more information your family doctor is given, the better able he will be to provide the care you need. If you are handed a letter from the hospital for your GP, make sure someone delivers it to him as soon as possible. Ask a relative or friend to telephone the doctor, write him a letter, or make an appointment with him, if you don't feel well enough to do so yourself and if you think there is important information he should know, or services you want from him quickly, such as a supply of tablets or a home visit. As a GP I certainly find it very helpful to be told that someone has just come out of hospital, and if relatives pass on information about the patient's current problems or needs I will often be able to sort them out far more quickly than if I have to wait for the hospital's discharge letter to arrive several days, or even weeks, later.

Some people would say all these questions and answers, all these efforts to communicate information, aren't important; as long as a person makes a good physical recovery from their illness that's all that matters. It's an argument I'm reluctant to accept, for it's been shown time and time again that relevant information given to patients actually helps them get better more quickly. Effective communication therefore needs to be regarded as a fundamental and very important part of a doctor's treatment. I believe medical care should offer more than pharmaceutical and technological wizardry. How sad if acute illness can bring a person close to death, but cannot bring them close to a doctor.

CHAPTER 8

CHRONIC ILLNESS

ILLNESS THAT PERSISTS for months or years has profound effects on sufferers and their families. Conditions such as diabetes, heart disease and asthma may or may not shorten life – in a medical sense the term chronic means simply 'long-lasting' – but even if the sufferer sees out his three score years and ten, the illness may significantly influence the quality of his existence. Not unnaturally, he may feel angry, resentful or depressed about his condition but, with a supportive family and adequate medical help, may be able to live a full and satisfying life despite it.

Good medical care can play a vital part in controlling a chronic disease and limiting its debilitating effects. Drugs, surgery, physiotherapy and other forms of treatment may be crucial in minimising the physical sequelae of the illness, but a person's relationship with their doctor (or doctors) is equally important in helping them to tackle the psychological problems which may go hand-in-hand with the disease. Unfortunately, the importance of this rapport between doctor and patient is often underestimated, and even when it is recognised, circumstances may conspire to prevent the relationship developing in such a way that it can provide the patient with much-needed support and understanding.

Medical care of chronic conditions is supervised both by GPs and hospital doctors. In the past the tendency was for a consultant to take over a patient's care if the GP referred them for an initial opinion or investigations. As the workload in many outpatient clinics increased, it became clear that they could not offer long-term follow-up to all their patients if they were also to continue providing a service for new referrals. In addition, it was also evident that some conditions could be looked after just as well by GPs, with less inconvenience to patients, so more and more long-term care of the chronically sick is now being dealt with in general practice. Most of this takes place in ordinary surgery time but some GPs have started special 'mini-clinics' for patients with diabetes, asthma or hypertension (high blood pressure) in the hope that by involving other health workers, such as nurses or dieticians, they can improve the efficiency and quality of their service to these patients.

Some people greatly prefer to be monitored by the GP rather than a hospital clinic. Ellen Spriggs, a frail but cheerful 71-year-old lady with rheumatoid arthritis, had been transferred from hospital to GP care six years ago.

'I never knew which doctor I'd see'

I was worried at first when the hospital said I was being discharged from their clinic back to my GP. I didn't know if she'd bother to see me every six months like they'd been doing, but she did. It's so much more convenient to get to her surgery – I don't have to wait for ambulances to take me and bring me back, and I rarely wait more than 20 minutes to see her whereas at the hospital I'd sometimes be sat for two hours before I was called. And I never knew which doctor I'd see there – so often it was someone I'd never met before. At least with my G P I know it'll always be her I see.

Not every patient is so enthusiastic about GP follow-up though. Sharon Miles, a bright girl in her early twenties who has had quite severe asthma since childhood, actually asked to be referred to a hospital specialist:

'They seem so much more clued up'

In my late teens the asthma got really bad. I seemed to be permanently wheezy and had to give up netball because any kind of exertion made it worse. I went to my G P several times and although he tried me on various sorts of tablets I didn't get any better. So I asked if he would send me to an asthma specialist and ever since then I've been under the hospital clinic. They seem so much more clued up about asthma there. They showed me how to use my inhalers properly and the doctors have used short courses of steroid tablets when I'm really bad which always gets me better in a few days.

Many hospital consultants see positive advantages in more chronic care being undertaken by GPs:

'We're only a back-up'

DR RUSSELL HITCHCOCK, THE MIDLANDS CHEST PHYSICIAN: I think we see far too many old patients who've been followed up by the hospital for too long. We don't give the responsibility to the GP and the patient suffers as a result because when he goes to his doctor with a problem the GP says, 'Oh, well, you're under the hospital so I can't do anything.' I think patients should be sent back to their GP as soon as possible if there isn't some special expertise that is required from us. They should feel that *he* is their doctor and we're only here as a back-up.

'That takes a big load off us'

MR RONALD LACEY, A CONSULTANT SURGEON IN WALES: We're trying to reduce the number of long-term follow-ups. We're lucky because, by and large, we've got really excellent general practitioners around here and unless the patient has something like a malignant disease we can discharge them straight back to the care of the GP. So we don't have to see large numbers of routine follow-ups as I used to when I was a senior registrar in the inner cities. That takes a big load off us and allows us to spend more time with the new patients and the ones with acute problems. I don't particularly mind not seeing patients long-term. If I'd wanted to keep in contact with patients and family groups I'd have been a general practitioner.

Doctors' attitudes to care of the chronically ill vary enormously. Almost everyone acknowledges that there are both difficulties and rewards inherent in this kind of work, but the way the balance tips seems to depend very much on the personality and interests of the individual doctor. Dr Jenny Scott, the gentle and sympathetic GP trainee in East London, had

152

encountered some of the problems of chronic care during her first year in general practice, but nonetheless had a very positive attitude towards it:

'90 per cent is to do with the relationship'

I rather enjoy looking after chronic illness. Of course, it depends what it is – in this borough a lot of chronic illness is linked to the environment and it's so difficult to do much about housing, about things like dampness and condensation, that sometimes you feel like you're fighting a losing battle. But if it's something like looking after the elderly then I enjoy that, because 90 per cent of the work is to do with the relationship between you – having a chat, finding out things, and feeling that they appreciate your interest. Most of the elderly people around here have lived in the borough a long time and I find it interesting hearing about what they saw in the War and how the place has changed. I think you can help in little ways, mainly by organising nursing care and by getting aids in the home that will make life slightly easier for them. It's much appreciated and makes quite a difference to the quality of their lives. Having said that, I think I have to be careful that I don't lapse into just having cosy chats and missing the medical problems. There's a danger when you see someone who's chronically sick that you get so used to them being in that state that you forget things.

Experienced GPs like Dr Tom Peterson tend to have more muted enthusiasm for chronic care:

'It's another challenge'

It's another challenge, another part of one's medical life. Much of the care of chronic illness is preventative care and if you can feel that you've prevented a condition getting worse or have prevented complications developing then there's a pay-off in it for you. Do I like it? Sometimes I do and sometimes I don't. I mean the person who is in misery and is determined to remain in misery is a misery for themselves and for me too, but the person who is brave is a joy.

'The illness is going to wear them down'

DR STEPHEN KERR: The trouble with chronic illness is that most of the things are degenerative and you know that there's going to be a slow and progressive deterioration over a matter of years which you can't really alter. One accepts that it's a very important part of general practice and probably an area that we're better at than many hospitals because we have a multi-disciplinary approach and can get help into the home from nurses, physiotherapists, occupational therapists and so on, so one can make life a good deal more tolerable for these people than it used to be. But you know, nevertheless, that at the end of the day the illness is going to wear them down and wear them out.

Because of the ongoing nature of chronic illness, one of the aspects of medical care which concerns patients most is continuity. With only one doctor responsible for their care, they can be sure that he is familiar with the details of their case, knows about past problems and is aware of their current treatment. The more often they see the same doctor, the more likely they are to trust him and feel relaxed with him. Such familiarity inspires confidence and good communication so that patients can air their problems and fears, and the doctor can be sure he is dealing with issues that are important to them.

It is difficult, if not impossible, for hospitals to provide this kind of continuity for patients because of the training requirements I have already outlined, which force junior doctors to move from job to job every six or twelve months. GPs, on the other hand, move around very little once they have established themselves in practice and so are more likely to provide the continuity that patients want and need.

Being able to provide this continuity is an aspect of general practice which I, and many other GPs, greatly enjoy. Patients make it clear how much they appreciate it, which is very satisfying for me, and I enjoy the 'social' side of the consultations – talking about family, holidays and suchlike – as much as they do. Such chatter is pleasant in itself but it's also vital in building up a picture of the person I'm treating, in order to understand their life and how it is affected by their illness.

I actually feel sorry for some of my patients who are still

154

under the hospital clinics for long-term follow-up rather than coming to me. That must sound terribly self-opinionated and I certainly don't mean to imply that I think I'm better than hospital doctors on the medical side of things. In fact, when it comes to consultants I know I lack a great deal of their expertise. But with many patients, the condition is fairly straightforward and so is its medical management, so they don't really need a specialist to look after them. What many of them do need though is someone they know and trust, who can talk with them about the effect of the disease on their work, or their marriage, or their self-esteem, and can help them find ways to solve these kinds of problems. I'd like to think that I can fulfil that kind of role for at least some of my patients.

There's a selfish side to it too. With some patients there isn't a great deal that you can do for them medically, and if I was an SHO in the out-patients clinic just seeing them once or twice during my six-month post I'd feel pretty inadequate because I'd have nothing to offer them. But to patients I know well I can give emotional support and a shoulder to cry on if they need it. Being able to do at least that much for them stops me from feeling helpless and impotent in the face of their relentless disease.

If GPs enjoy the element of continuity in their care of the chronic sick, do hospital doctors, who experience it far less, feel they are missing out? Many consultants say not, for they get some sense of continuity with patients, albeit superficial, by looking at their hospital notes and finding out, from what other doctors have written, how they're getting on. Although this may be enough to give the consultant a sense of keeping in touch, it rarely gives patients the kind of personal attention they would like. Dr Robertson, the gastroenterology consultant in a Midlands hospital, described how he tried to deal with the problem:

'I do look at the notes each time'

With regard to the old patients, clearly I can't see all of them. But I do like to know what's going on, so when I look through the pile of notes at each out-patient clinic even if I haven't seen a particular patient myself I can see from the various comments that my juniors have written that all's going well. Sometimes the nurses have to explain to patients that although they may not see me very often, I do look at the notes each time they come to the clinic and if I was unhappy with how things were progressing I would see them the next time. In fact, if they're seen by the SHO it usually means that I'm very satisfied with how they're going along and so am happy for them to be seen by a junior doctor, but sometimes the nurses do have to explain that to them because they complain that they never see the consultant. It's difficult to get that across to everyone. The nurse will explain it to the occasional person, but I'm sure lots of patients would like to know that if they come along to a clinic and are seen by a different SHO every six months it doesn't mean they're totally forgotten and that nobody's concerned about them.

'It's impossible to give a personalised service'

DR MORRIS, THE YOUNG CONSULTANT WHO SPECIALISED IN THE CARE OF DIABETES: I'm afraid it's impossible to give patients a personalised service. The only thing I can do is make sure I see all the notes before each clinic, so that I can decide who will see me and who will see the other doctors. What I tend to do is see people with difficult problems who I think need my attention, and those with more routine problems I'll see on about one visit in every three. At least by thumbing through the notes I can make sure that no one's been coming to the clinic for ten years and hasn't seen a consultant, and hopefully can tell that there are no major problems that I ought to be involving myself with. The only way round the problem is with more money – more money to employ more consultants so we could share out the workload.

The bigger the hospital, the more junior staff it will employ, and the less likely patients are to see the same doctor at each clinic visit. Small hospitals, or small departments within large hospitals, are often staffed by a consultant and only one or two juniors, and although they may not be able to provide patients with the most sophisticated equipment or spacious facilities, they can often give a more personal service. Dr Kumara, a consultant in a small radiotherapy unit in the Midlands, described the advantages of such a set-up:

'Seeing the patient all the way through is much more satisfying'

I just have the one SHO working for me and she looks after the wards, so I do all the out-patient work by myself. Now that I have complete clinical responsibility for each patient, see them at every visit and follow them through the entire course of the illness, I've got to know the patients much more. I get to see the relatives and know the social background. That's made the patients much more real to me than, say, three or four years ago. I may be making a virtue out of necessity, but I do think that by keeping one's finger on the pulse and seeing the patient all the way through, it's much more satisfying for the doctor, and for the patient as well. I wouldn't have it any other way.

Mr Dougal Cameron also ran his out-patient clinics (in paediatric surgery) largely on his own:

'Old friends come back'

There are two reasons for that. Firstly, there aren't all that many rooms, and secondly, well, it's just the way I'm used to practising. I don't know whether the parents appreciate it, but they certainly get better continuity of care this way. It's quicker in one sense because if a patient has a thick set of case notes I'll know what's gone on before, whereas another doctor would have to start wading through them to find out what's happened in the past. It's satisfying too. There are some old friends who come back every now and again and I think we both enjoy seeing one another. It certainly means I can monitor their progress more closely.

An ongoing relationship between doctor and patient might seem to pave the way for mutual satisfaction, but continuity of care is not without potential disadvantages, at least in doctors' eyes. There is always the possibility that a patient looked after by just one doctor will become overly reliant on them. George Peters had a heart attack when he was 48 and saw his GP regularly for several months afterwards. Gradually he became dependent on the doctor's repeated reassurance and advice, although he found this difficult to acknowledge:

'I feel better once I've had a chat'

I was devastated by the heart attack, terrified that it would happen again. The GP was great though. He saw me every couple of weeks to check my blood pressure and see whether I needed to change the tablets I was taking. I still get chest pains even now, a year later, and I've had to call him out several times. He says it's nothing to do with my heart – it's just me getting worked up – and my wife says the same thing. She's even told me I ought to set up home at the doctor's surgery because I'm down there so often, but I think it's better to be safe than sorry. I just feel better once I've had a chat with the doctor.

Strange though it may seem, a patient's gratitude may become a burden to the doctor for he may feel obliged to treat the patient as special in some way in order to return their affection. The safe boundaries of the professional relationship may become blurred, causing the doctor to feel distinctly uncomfortable. Mr Millington, the paediatric surgeon, had experienced this kind of situation with the mother of one of his patients:

'You're thinking about them all the time'

One of my patients, Michael, is a child of about six who has terrible kidneys. He's going to need a lot of surgery at some stage but all I've done so far is a simple procedure which has managed to improve his kidney function. His mother will only come to see *me* in the clinic and she knows that from time to time I may be away for a meeting, or because of teaching commitments, so she always telephones my secretary the day before to find out if I'll be doing the clinic because if I'm not, she won't come.

On one occasion I was going away on holiday for a month and she phoned me up the day before to say, 'I just thought you'd like to know that Michael is well and doesn't have any infection in his urine, in case you were going to be worrying about him over the next month.' That made me realise just how much she thought of me, and what sort of position she put me in. Parents like her believe that their child is the only patient you're treating, and that you're thinking about them all the time.

Somehow this mother found out when my birthday is, so every year she sends me a birthday card and at Christmas she gives me a present. Last year when I saw Michael in the clinic I realised it was his birthday a few days later so I sent him a birthday card, but I forgot to do it this year. That must be a terrible blow to his mother but I think it's wrong that I should find myself in a position where I feel I ought to be sending a birthday card. She can do it if she likes, but I shouldn't be getting that involved.

The ease with which a doctor finds a balance between professional detachment and personal involvement has a lot to do with his personality. Some, like Dr Dick Hamilton, do not shy away from becoming involved with patients, even though it may cause them heartache at times.

‘That can make things difficult’

I see quite a few children with end-stage renal [kidney] failure. Some of them are now seven and eight and I've been looking after them since they were six or seven months old. I see them once a month, so I've got to know their parents and in some cases I'm godfather to one of their brothers or sisters. I've got to know those families very, very well indeed and yes, that can make things difficult for me at times. For example, a boy came in last year and had a kidney transplant which rejected. That sort of thing's quite traumatic when you're involved to the extent that I'm involved.

Another problem for doctors who take on sole responsibility for patients is that they must shoulder the burden of medical care completely on their own. Sometimes this can be very stressful, particularly if the patient's condition deteriorates despite treatment, or if they feel dissatisfied with the doctor's management, and say so! The doctor's distress may, however, be minimal compared to the patient's, and if you consider a doctor's care to be unsatisfactory there are steps you can take to improve matters.

Although you may find it awkward to do so, the best thing is to talk to the doctor concerned about your grievances. You may feel angry with him, but it won't help to show it. Doctors, like most other people, tend to become more defensive and less cooperative when under verbal attack! If, after a rational discussion, you still feel dissatisfied, the next step depends on whether you are dealing with a GP or a hospital doctor. With a GP, you can either try asking for a second opinion (from a hospital consultant) or consider changing to a different general practitioner. If you feel you have grounds for complaint against your GP you should put these in writing to your local Family Practitioner Committee if you live in England or Wales, to the Secretary of the Health Board in Scotland, and in Northern Ireland to the Chief Administrative Officer of the Health and Social Services Board. In hospital, if you're unhappy with a junior doctor, ask to speak to the consultant, and if you're already dealing with 'the boss' himself, and do not feel happier after discussing things with him, then ask if he will refer you to another consultant. If you know you'll find it difficult to express your dissatisfaction when you're face-to-face with the doctor, then write everything down clearly beforehand and ask him to read your notes. Often tactics like this will make the doctor realise that he has not communicated well with you so far, and will remind him to make a particular effort to explain things to you clearly in the future.

When a patient feels dissatisfied with a doctor's management of their condition it often helps if there is someone else already involved in their care who can step in and give a second opinion. For this reason shared-care schemes between hospitals and GPs often work very well. With diabetics, for example, a hospital consultant and GP will jointly decide what kind of follow-up is needed and how this can be shared between them. If the patient sees the GP every three months and attends the hospital diabetic clinic once a year, he gets continuity from his family doctor but has easy access to an alternative source of help and advice should he want it. Such a system also makes it easier for hospital doctors and GPs to share the overall workload of chronic care as well as any particular concerns about individual patients.

Anyone suffering from a chronic illness has somehow to cope with it, or adapt to it, if it is not to overshadow their life. Understanding the disease – its cause, its physical and mental effects, and the rationale behind the treatment prescribed – is crucial if a person wants to share in the medical management of the condition and avoid being completely dependent on doctors. For their part, doctors must be willing to let patients take as much responsibility for their own well-being as they want, and feel able, to cope with. The process of educating patients about their disease and its management is time-consuming, but one which many doctors enjoy:

'They soon learn'

DR JENNY SCOTT: I like drawing diagrams or explaining to people what is actually going on physically and how to use their drugs most effectively. That's very enjoyable because once you give people responsibility they are much better at managing their illness than you are, or they soon learn to be. I'm here if they need me for advice or they want to see me about other things, but I think the more people manage and know about their own conditions the better.

'Responsibility should be on the patient'

DR RUSSELL HITCHCOCK: A disease like asthma is the sort of disease in which the patient needs educating. There have been enormous strides in helping patients to understand their asthma and we can do an enormous amount for an asthmatic's confidence in their therapy and in themselves. We can give them peak-flow meters[1] so they can record measurements regularly and can see how their treatment's working and how much they need. In an uncomplicated asthmatic I think the responsibility should be very much on the patient to make sure they treat themselves properly.

Doctors don't always find it easy to be honest with patients about their disease and so help them to understand it more fully. Sometimes they appear secretive and patronising, as one 40-year-old woman I spoke to in a Derby hospital had found:

'I wish he'd told me straight away'

I was sent up to out-patients first of all by my GP because I'd noticed some bleeding when I went to the toilet. The doctor I saw looked inside the back passage with a tube and told me I'd

1. A peak-flow meter is a hand-held device which a patient blows into. A scale on the device indicates how narrowed the airways to their lungs are, and so gives the patient with asthma an idea of how well his treatment is working.

161

have to have a barium X-ray test on the bowel, but it would be a week or so before that could be done. I was out of my mind with worry, thinking it might be cancer, but when I asked him if it was he just said, 'Don't you worry now. We'll sort it out whatever it is.' I was sure he must've seen something nasty when he looked down the tube, but he didn't tell me anything and I was too frightened to ask. It turned out I was right. He had seen a growth but he didn't tell me until I saw him two weeks later. I actually felt relieved once I knew for certain what was wrong and I just wish he'd told me straight away that he'd thought it was cancer.

In a situation like that, a doctor's attitude may be fuelled more by a desire to minimise the patient's anxiety, than by any deliberate wish to keep them in the dark. An incident which occurred while I was talking with Dr Morris illustrates the point. The wife of one of his patients, a newly diagnosed diabetic in his sixties, telephoned to ask about her husband's latest blood result. After she had rung off Dr Morris reflected on what he had told her:

'Patients can't take it'

She asked the question, 'Is his diabetes bad?' Well, what do you say? He had a blood sugar level of 28 yesterday. I felt I had to say, 'No, it's not bad.' 'Is it mild?' she asked, and I said, 'Yes,' even though it's not. If I'd said anything else she'd have gone away worrying on his behalf. Apparently her husband's always been a twitched sort of chap and now that he's got diabetes there's no way he won't be twitched about that, whatever you tell him. I think we have to be realistic here and accept the fact that because of his anxiety there can never be open communication between us. People talk about the fact that doctors don't tell the truth. Well, one of the reasons we sometimes don't is because patients can't take it. They really can't.

It can also be difficult for doctors to get the balance right when trying to share responsibility for treatment with a patient. Sometimes we are too paternalistic, and anger people by failing to include them in the process of decision-making. Other patients, who are often older and in awe of the medical profession, seem unnerved by the prospect of any medical responsibility and prefer to leave decisions to the doctor. If we get used to telling this sort of patient what to do, it's all too easy to behave in the same way with many others as well, although we may convince ourselves that they are making their own decisions. Dr Anthony Hall, the forceful rheumatology and rehabilitation consultant, spoke about 'guiding' his patients, but I found myself wondering how much the term was a euphemism for gentle coercion:

What I like to do is offer options and, depending on the sort of reception I get, guide. Some people need more pushing than guidance, but I do prefer people to make their own decisions.

'We shouldn't play God'

MR RONALD LACEY: Younger people want to know a lot more about their condition or their disease. They take a lot more interest in the decisions to be made and that's excellent. As for the elderly, well, we're always told that we shouldn't play God and tell people what's right and wrong, but often it's difficult not to with older people because they don't want to know, or can't make the decision. They throw things back to us and say, 'You decide, I'll do what you say,' so sometimes we're forced into that role.

Although doctors profess to welcoming patients' growing self-reliance, I'm sure that many of us would be alarmed if they felt able to dispense with our help altogether. We are trained to assume a directive role in medical care, and so like to believe that our opinions and advice will always be valued by patients, even when they have achieved a measure of medical independence. I think doctors have a real need to be needed, and we therefore feel rejected and useless if patients seem able to manage their illness without our help. As Mr Millington said of feeling indispensable, 'It's a drug, and being a doctor gets me my regular "fix".'

163

It doesn't surprise me that doctors want people to need them; we chose, after all, to enter a 'caring profession' which gives us the opportunity to be a rock for others to cling to. The role is a legitimate one too, for society needs people who are willing and able to help the sick; what it could do without is doctors' rigid view of their own role, especially with regard to chronic illness – the emphasis on physical aspects of disease in medical training which makes doctors prone to tunnel vision when considering patients' needs. We have no trouble focusing on their physical problems, but the psychological and social consequences of disease hover on the edge of our visual fields, indistinct and easily ignored.

One of the things I find most difficult as a doctor is to stop being just that – a doctor – and instead put myself in a patient's shoes in order to appreciate the effect that a chronic illness has on their life. Take psoriasis, for example. It's a common disorder which produces red patches on the skin. These shed silvery scales and, in severe cases, can cover huge areas of the body. Ray Jobling, himself a psoriasis sufferer, has written clearly about how those with the condition are affected by it:

There is no doubt that however unjustifiable in rational, factual terms, those with psoriasis do feel ashamed, guilty and in some cases deeply disturbed. . . . Asked the worst thing about having psoriasis, sufferers repeatedly respond in clear terms.

Revulsion against one's body and a feeling of never really being clean.

(Man, 69 years, psoriasis for 20 years)

One always feels unclean. In my young days I would never expose myself to view.

(Woman, 53 years, psoriasis for 30 years)

I have always felt a sense of shame. I feel it most when I look at my body. I try to hide it even from friends, especially from friends in fact. But the scales make it difficult. It is such a dirty disease.

(Woman, 70 years, psoriasis for 12 years)[2]

2. Jobling, R., 'The Experience of Psoriasis Under Treatment' in *Living With Chronic Illness*, Anderson, R., and Bury, M. (eds), Unwin Hyman, 1988; pp 225–44.

164

A doctor diligently trying to improve a patient's psoriasis may view the problem in mainly physical terms and so will see only a troubled skin and not the troubled person inside it. To be fully aware of the condition as the sufferer experiences it, the doctor must acknowledge not just the nature of the skin abnormality but also the wider problems it creates for the person affected. To do so is often difficult for doctors; issues such as the social stigma of skin disease and a patient's perception of their condition as a form of punishment are far more complex to deal with than the skin lesions themselves. With the physical manifestations of psoriasis the doctor is comforted by the belief that his intervention will have at least some beneficial effect. The social and psychological problems may seem far more threatening to him, for there are no ready solutions that he can provide. Unconsciously he may avoid broaching these subjects with the patient for fear that having done so he will have no useful remedy to offer.

On my travels around the country interviewing doctors, I also spoke to a number of their patients. Some of them expressed anger and frustration at doctors' inability to appreciate anything other than the purely medical effects of chronic illness on their lives. One embittered young man was Gary Austin, a small, wiry fellow with bleached blond hair, who had suffered from diabetes since the age of 11.

'I couldn't handle it'

I had a bit of a problem with doctors during my teens. They didn't really explain the diabetes to me. Well, they talked all about the medical side of it, but didn't explain the psychological side of it. It was really bad having to inject meself with insulin. It seemed as if I had to inflict pain on meself. They didn't explain anything about that to me and it's very hard to accept, especially when you're 11. I think they put too much on my shoulders. I was supposed to control the diabetes and do all these blood tests and so on and so forth. One minute I was a perfectly fit lad of 11, and then all of a sudden I'm told I'm diabetic and had needles coming at me from all over the place. I couldn't handle it.

Because of his difficulty in coming to terms with the diabetes and with his abhorrence of injections, Gary often refused to have his daily insulin treatment. As a result, his diabetes was poorly controlled for many years, and complications, including damaged eyesight, ensued. Although he accepts that it was his own failure to take insulin that caused the subsequent problems, he was angry that doctors had not tried harder to find out *why* he was failing to comply with treatment.

'They just thought I was being awkward'

All I can remember about diabetes in childhood was me mum saying, 'Have you had your needle?' and me lying about it, saying, 'Yes, I've had it.' I knew darned well that I hadn't but I couldn't bring meself to take it. The doctors didn't ask, didn't want to know why I wasn't turning up at clinics and wasn't taking the insulin. They just thought I was being an awkward case. A lot of the 'old-school' type of doctors treated you like a spoilt child. They'd tell you what you were doing wrong and correct you, and if you still didn't do it right they'd stick it for so long and then just wash their hands of you.

In the last few years Gary had begun to take his insulin more regularly and so had found doctors less hectoring. He still felt, however, that the consultant who had taken over his care two years before did not really understand the effect of the diabetes, its treatment and the need for continuous monitoring, on his life.

'Life is nothing but injections'

A doctor's version of diabetic control, and my version of control are quite different. They're always worrying about what the blood sugar level is but I think that even if it's fine, if the insulin is ruling your life then there's no point to it because you haven't got a life. There has to be a happy balance between the sugar being OK and being able to live a decent life. It can get to the point where life is nothing but injections and weekly visits to the diabetic clinic. It's all diabetes-orientated. Everything. You get sick of it. Really fed up with it.

Although Gary had become quite confident about managing his diabetes he was still keen to get help from doctors, and his relationship with them was obviously important to him. Going to the hospital clinic was still something of an ordeal though, even after 14 years as a diabetic, and there were several reasons why he often came away disappointed.

'You become a number not a patient'

Doctors don't seem to understand that waiting for hours in the clinic makes you fretful and nervous. And if you're going to the clinic week in and week out, you've got that anguish and nervousness every week. Doctors don't realise the upheaval it causes to the people they're treating.

I have to go to the Eye Clinic for laser treatment now, and that's like a conveyor belt. When you first go to a new clinic you're OK, you're dealt with as a patient. But after a while, it may take four or five visits, you become a number, not a patient. My mother, who's also diabetic, feels it particularly – you know, feels they don't care.

With Dr Franks, the consultant I had for yeaars, when I went to see him he seemed to concentrate on me and my problems. I don't know my new consultant that well, but when I see him he's like a bee buzzing around, always rushing off to see another patient. I don't know if he's overloaded or hyperactive or what, but I can't handle it. If a doctor concentrates on just you while you're with him it gives you a sense of security. You know that your problem's being dealt with and you'll open up a lot more. If you're talking to a doctor and he has to disappear, by the time he comes back you feel all inhibited again and you're not interested in talking any more.

When I come to the Diabetic Clinic I know there's an 80 per cent chance that I won't see the consultant so he doesn't really know me. The other week he had to fill in a form about me and he didn't even know there was anything wrong with my eyesight. I know he's got a big workload but something like that makes you feel you can't have any confidence in him, or share any real problems with him. What you need is a doctor who knows you, and knows your problems.

Gary's case illustrates well the need for good communication between a doctor and patient in order for medical care to be of real benefit to someone with a chronic illness. This does not simply mean sharing our medical knowledge with patients; to be effective, communication has to be a two-way process, so it is imperative that patients share their knowledge, and experience, of the disease with us. The thorny problem for doctors and patients is how to amalgamate their very different images of a chronic disorder. A doctor's picture of disease revolves around symptoms, physical signs and laboratory results; for a patient, the disease affects not only their body but their mind, their family, their work and leisure, and numerous other aspects of their life. As a result, the patient and doctor may have very different goals for treatment; goals which conflict and cause misunderstanding, frustration and resentment on both sides. Dr Morris described the communication problem as he saw it:

'The patient sees his illness, the consultant a collection of symptoms'

I think there's a major problem of difference in perspective between patient and consultant. The patient sees his illness, and only his illness, in the context of his life. What the consultant often sees is a collection of symptoms, or perhaps test abnormalities, which are seen in the context of medicine, and I think that patients and consultants don't necessarily understand that they are coming together with totally different viewpoints. It's not surprising that I don't understand the way the patient feels and it's no more surprising that the patient doesn't understand what I feel. Sometimes when I ask the most basic of questions like, 'Have you ever felt your pulse?' and the patient hasn't, I realise just how far away many people are from knowing the first thing about what I'm saying. So even though we do our best to try and put things across in a way that fits patients' own perceptions of their illness, we may be a million miles from that, and I think we usually are. At the moment I'm not certain whether that gulf can be bridged, given the constraints that I think we operate under.

Dr Morris is right that there is sometimes little understanding between doctors and patients, but I feel more optimistic than he does about the ability of doctors (at least in the long term) to appreciate and respond to patients' view of disease. This issue is probably the biggest stumbling block on the road to better communication between doctors and patients, but all the problems of chronic care cannot be attributed to the disparity between medical and lay concepts of illness. Practical issues play a part as well – for instance, the difficulty of providing continuity of care whilst satisfying junior doctors' training requirements – and these may not be easy for the individual doctor or patient to remedy. What they can both do is try and bridge the gulf between their respective worlds, for in so doing they would discover that they are allies, not adversaries, in the battle against chronic disability.

CHAPTER 9

DEATH AND DYING

THE CERTAINTY THAT, one day, all of us will die makes it no easier to come to terms with our mortality during life. Sex may have been Victorian society's taboo subject, but death is undoubtedly ours. We don't like to think about it, let alone discuss it, and now that death has ceased to be part of our communal experience, many of us go through life without ever seeing a dead body. Corpses are swiftly veiled with sheets then whisked away to be entombed in coffins, so the living need not contemplate the stark reality of death.

For doctors, death is an unavoidable part of work. Although we have become more skilled at combating disease and prolonging life we have yet to find the key to immortality, so for every baby born into the world there will inevitably be another death certificate to sign. During their careers doctors may become familiar with the business of dying, but their upbringing saddles them with the same attitudes and inhibitions as everyone else; attitudes and inhibitions which influence them when they deal with death in a professional capacity.

In the same way that birth has become 'medicalised' over the centuries, so dying has become a process which people are frightened to face without doctors' assistance. Three-quarters of the population now die in hospital – a reflection of the fear, inadequacy and distaste which the prospect of death engenders both in those who are dying and in their families. Since medical involvement is so commonplace when death approaches, you might expect doctors to be skilled at dealing with the problems it poses for patients and relatives. Sadly, this is rarely the case, and at a time when doctor and patient could become closer, they often find themselves distanced by mutual awkwardness and fear.

Richard Marks, a 40-year-old businessman, described how he had been told that his wife had a brain tumour which could not be treated.

'He seemed very uncomfortable'

The doctor took me off to the ward office and sat me down there. He seemed very uncomfortable, as if he wanted to get the business over and done with as quickly as possible. He told me straight out that Jan had a brain tumour which would probably kill her in the next six months. He said there wasn't much they could do to prolong her life, but if we wanted them to, they'd try. I was so stunned I couldn't say anything. I think he found the silence embarrassing because he kept saying, 'Do you have any questions?' and when I couldn't think of any he immediately said, 'I'm sorry, I have to go now,' and left.

Coping with dying patients and relatives can be especially hard for young, inexperienced doctors. Robbie Kendall, the SHO on a paediatric ward in Edinburgh, told me about his feelings of inadequacy when faced with a dying child.

'I don't have a clue'

It's very difficult. I don't really have a clue what to say to the parents. I can think of an example recently when a child I knew moderately well was dying. The consultant had said nothing else could be done, and the child was being left to die overnight. As I passed his room I thought of going in to speak to the parents but I couldn't bring myself to do it because I thought it would be so awkward and I wouldn't be able to say anything of value. I was afraid there'd be an embarrassing silence with me standing about not knowing what to say.

Most doctors find their first few encounters with dying patients particularly stressful. Dr Tessa Collins, the young houseman I met in North Wales, was no exception; one of the difficulties she encountered during her first three months on the wards was handling her own emotional response to the near-death of a patient.

171

'I was desperate'

There was one occasion when a chap came in who'd arrested in
the GP's surgery and I got to know him really well – a pet
patient really. He recovered and went home and then one night
when we were on call he came back to hospital with more chest
pain. I was sitting at the desk and somebody shouted that he'd
arrested in the side room. I found I was shaking when I got
there. In a way I felt much more agitated and less in control of
the situation because it was a patient I knew well. I was desperate
I suppose. I thought, We've *got* to bring him round. We did
resuscitate him, but afterwards we thought he might be brain
damaged and when we told his wife she said, 'If he arrests again
I don't want him to be resuscitated,' and I just burst into floods
of tears. He did become rouseable later though, and when I went
to see him I said, 'Do you know who I am?' and he said, 'Yes,
Tessa, tell me what's happened,' and oh, my goodness, I felt
really emotional then.

Medical students, like other people in their twenties, are too
busy enjoying life to contemplate death seriously. Many will
have had no experience of close relatives or friends dying and
few will have thought through the practical, emotional and
spiritual issues that death brings with it. Despite this un-
preparedness, young doctors have to deal with dying patients
from the day they qualify, and only then do many realise how
ill-equipped they are to cope with the situation.

In my second year as an SHO I worked for six months with
leukaemia patients and part of my job was to care for people
having bone marrow transplants. Many of these patients had
relapsed after initial drug therapy for their leukaemia and without the transplant they were destined to die. Even with the
procedure their future was uncertain; we knew that many
would not survive the transplant itself and of those who did,
some would still succumb to complications or recurrent leukaemia.

Preparation for a bone marrow transplant is not a pleasant
business: patients must undergo total body irradiation and
potent chemotherapy, both of which can cause distressing side
effects. The transplant itself is painless for the recipient – a
simple infusion of fluid into a vein – but for weeks afterwards

they are vulnerable to infections and other complications which may cause pain, weakness and other unpleasant symptoms. Every day I watched people suffer this ordeal in the hope of beating their leukaemia. Some were my age, and even younger, enduring a physical and mental torture which I could barely comprehend. Many lost their struggle for life and each tragic, death I witnessed added to the grey cloud of despondency hanging over my head.

Although the job was incredibly busy, little of my time was spent talking with patients. I checked their physical condition every day but leisurely chats were few and far between; routine tasks like clerking in new patients, administering drugs, chasing and filing results, taking blood specimens and attending ward rounds took up most of my time, so patients and their families received far less of my attention than I thought they should. Despite the gravity of their illness I felt distanced from many patients and was both puzzled and frustrated by my failure to build close relationships with them.

One of the leukaemia patients I looked after was a gentle and introspective man in his early twenties called Michael. Although he was the proud father of a baby girl, he had never been able to kiss or cuddle her because he had to be nursed in a special isolation cubicle following the bone marrow transplant he received just a few days before his daughter was born. Michael desperately wanted to live but for weeks after the transplant he remained very ill; when he overcame one complication, another developed, and the fear in his eyes told me only too clearly that he could see his own death approaching and was terrified at the prospect.

I felt that as a doctor I should be able to comfort and support him but I was terrified too. With no training in how to care for dying patients I felt inadequate and my own fear made it impossible for me to be a source of strength to him. When Michael died I was smitten with guilt, convinced that I had failed both him and his girlfriend because of my inability to offer them the emotional support they needed. That guilt has since turned to anger – anger at a system which teaches doctors how to cure but not how to care, and encourages them to prize life but recoil from death. Traditional medical training leaves doctors ill-prepared for terminal care, so that many find it impossible to meet the needs of dying patients.

There are many reasons why doctors perform badly in the face of terminal illness, not least of which is the feeling of impotence it can evoke. Our training provides us with the knowledge and skills to make sick people well again. The drugs and technology at our disposal reinforce our self-image as healers. But when faced with a disease we cannot overcome, we find ourselves stripped of the curative role with which we have grown comfortable. Our desire to intervene and pursue 'active' management must be quelled, and comfort rather than cure should become our first concern. Many doctors find it difficult to accept such passivity in the face of disease and the impotence, frustration or anger they feel may unconsciously be vented on the very patient who needs their help.

Terminal or palliative care is, in fact, far from passive; doctors specialising in this field are actively involved with their patients' treatment, but the emphasis for them is not on cure but on care. That care attends not only to physical needs, but emotional, spiritual and social ones too, and it embraces family and friends closely involved with the patient. 'Medicine' of this kind demands time and sensitivity from a doctor and is a form of care many find difficult to give.

Dr John Blackmore, the medical director of a hospice in the west of England, had this to say of doctors' inability to provide satisfactory terminal care:

'Nobody tells you that love is important'

Nothing in medical training teaches you that care in the emotional sense has anything to do with being a doctor. Nobody actually tells undergraduates that love, in the sort of way that I'm talking about it – really caring about how the patient feels and thinks – should be important to you, and that learning how to communicate is also important, no matter what sort of doctor you're going to be. When I was at medical school there was never anything mentioned about death and dying so I had no clues about it at all. I had no example to follow because the people I remember dying were, by and large, ignored by consultants.

Dr Blackmore reiterated a point I have discussed in previous chapters – that as medical science and technology have mushroomed, so doctors' ability to understand and empathise with people has dwindled. The human element of medical care has become swamped by the knowledge and practical skills we have acquired. In our dogged determination to find the cause and cure for every ill, patients have become the object of our intellectual interest rather than our human concern.

'Medicine has become more scientific'

DR BLACKMORE: As the years have gone by, medicine has become more scientific, more exciting, more thrilling. We're doing increasingly expensive and dramatic things like lung transplants, and there are more and more skilled things you can do to help people in increasingly rare situations, but there's nothing that gives you any clue as to the priority you should give to the people who are *not* going to get better. There doesn't seem to be any particular kudos attached to being good at terminal care, and doctors do seek kudos from their work. It's also impossible to measure 'success' in terminal care because you can't quantify it, and in modern-day medicine and surgery everyone wants to measure everything.

As diagnostic and therapeutic techniques have grown increasingly complex and sophisticated, hospital medicine has become more adventurous and exhilarating. Even doctors who go into general practice or other community work receive their basic training in hospitals, so it is hospital attitudes that we are all exposed to as highly impressionable students. Reared on a diet of exciting detective work, bold decisions and effective intervention, many doctors find the gradual and predictable deterioration of terminally ill patients too dull to warrant their attention. This is doctor-centred medicine at its worst, but only by acknowledging its lure can doctors take steps to suppress it and put patients' needs before their own. Dr Blackmore had been a GP for many years before moving into the field of hospice care and, with hindsight, was aware that he had experienced this kind of conflict himself.

'A dying patient deserved time'

I look back on my time in general practice and I realise I was
very egotistical. Nothing had trained me to think that a dying
patient actually deserved as much time as the one I was going to
cure. I was primarily concerned with *my* sense of satisfaction and
in doing things I found interesting. I can easily see the difference
between me as a doctor then and me as a doctor now. I'm less
interested in my self-satisfaction and importance now, and much
more interested, hopefully in an unselfish way, in how I've been
able to help the patient and the family. I think that's a big
difference.

Putting their own professional satisfaction before the needs of
patients is not the only reason why some doctors avoid the
dying. When cure rather than care is seen as the ultimate goal
of medicine, doctors often feel they've failed if they cannot
eradicate a patient's disease. Cancer and other incurable illnesses
force doctors to admit they're not invincible, and dying patients
may be dismayed when they realise this too. For doctors accustomed to admiration and awe it is an uncomfortable fall
from grace, and one which they unconsciously try to avoid by
detaching themselves from the dying patient and their family.

Dealing with dying patients is threatening for most doctors.
Usually we feel confident of having all the answers – or at least
knowing where to go to find them – but terminally ill patients
pose questions which defy glib replies. 'How will I die?', 'How
long have I got?', 'Will God forgive me?', or 'Why me?' We can
rarely give an authoritative answer and must be prepared to
say, 'I don't know.' The prospect is unsettling for many doctors;
they feel vulnerable without their shield of omniscience to
protect them, and may shy away from a situation which leaves
them so uncomfortably exposed.

It's hardly surprising that doctors encounter so many difficulties in caring for the dying, for they are neither born, nor
trained, for the job. Virtually every young doctor I spoke to felt
that the important issues surrounding death and dying had
been neglected at medical school, leaving them to muddle their
way through the problems when faced with terminally ill
patients after they'd qualified.

'No one helps you at all'

DR GRAHAM HUNT: I always seem to get landed with the job of
telling cancer patients their diagnosis. The nurses won't do it and
since the registrar's rarely around I have to tell them. It's been
really bad because no one tells you how to do it. Medical school
was completely useless in that way. I've had to find my own
system of doing it, through bitter experience.

GR: Did you find it difficult?

'I got taught nothing about dying'

DR GRAHAM HUNT: Yes, awful. Dreadful. No one helps you at all.
You just have to get on and do it.
DR HELEN BADCOCK: I think terminal care's a very important and a
very neglected part of medicine. As a student I got taught nothing
about people dying. At first I found it incredibly difficult to be
the bearer of bad news. I don't know whether anyone could
have done anything to make it easier, but I do think we should
have had more guidance on how to talk to people who are
dying. It's not as difficult now as it was at first. I'm not as
awkward, but it's still not easy.

'I just didn't know what to say'

DR TESSA COLLINS: I think I'm fairly communicative and I don't
find it difficult to talk to patients on the whole. But having to tell
people that a relative has died, that's something I found no one
had prepared me for. The first time I had to tell a wife that her
husband had died I found it awful. I just didn't know what to
say.
  I don't like having to tell people that they've got cancer either.
I worry about whether I should tell them or not, and I must
admit I often leave it to somebody else to tell them. You see we
had these esoteric things in medical school like sociology tutorials
telling you about care of the dying, but nobody actually gave us
a few ideas of what to say.

  Care of the dying has received scant attention in medical
student training. Since Dame Cicely Saunders pioneered the

hospice movement some 20 years ago, there has been only a slow acceptance by the medical profession of the importance and effectiveness of skilled terminal care, and, as a result, medical schools have devoted little curriculum time to teaching students about the subject. Now, at long last, there are signs of change.

In 1988 I sent a questionnaire to all UK medical schools and the replies revealed that three were spending more than ten hours dealing with terminal care during the five-year course, 17 devoted between two and ten hours to the subject and four gave no specific teaching in this area at all (three medical schools did not answer the questionnaire). The majority were therefore giving relatively little attention to this difficult area, but several of the schools were in the process of making changes to the curriculum which would include more time for the teaching of terminal care as a specific subject.

Things seem to be moving in the right direction but it's essential that all medical schools, not just a minority, include this area as a standard part of training if we are to hope for better care of the dying from the doctors of tomorrow. The new teaching will have to focus on patients' emotional and spiritual needs, as well as their physical problems, if it is to be successful, and medical students must be helped to prepare for an area of doctoring which they themselves may find difficult and distressing.

One issue that medical students certainly need help to grapple with is that of potential conflict between their personal feelings and their professional role. Any doctor caring for a dying patient responds to them on a human and a professional level. These two components of caring may be so intertwined as to be inseparable, but many of the doctors I talked with admitted to some conflict between the two, usually because of fears that their emotional reactions might in some way compromise their professional care for the patient.

'Patients expect you to be strong'

DR TESSA COLLINS: Sometimes I can stand back and if a patient or

relative breaks down I can cope, and there are other times when
I'm more involved that I'm frightened I'll break down as well.

GR: Why are you worried that you might break down? Is it simply
because you don't like crying in front of anybody, or do you
feel 'I'm supposed to be a doctor, I'm supposed to be the strong
one'?

DR TESSA COLLINS: I suppose it's a bit of both really. I do feel
embarrassed about showing too much emotion and also I
think patients expect you to be strong. I feel they might react
adversely to me bursting into tears. They might lose confidence
in me.

Mr Dougal Cameron, the consultant paediatric surgeon, was
in his sixties. His dour Scots exterior hid a wry sense of humour:

'There's got to be someone who's not crumbling'

MR DOUGAL CAMERON: I think we all find it difficult speaking to
parents who have just lost a child. They will often show their
grief quite visibly, but I would try not to.

GR: Do you think that's a coping mechanism for you?

MR DOUGAL CAMERON: Well, I'm a Presbyterian you see, that's
what it is. It's my inhibitions. I wouldn't sit down and cry with
parents. I think that's inappropriate. I don't know anyone who
does. Mind you, that might be the right thing to do. If you had a
wee grief session together that might make them feel better. I
can express my sorrow but I would try and control it, and it's not
all that difficult if you keep a little separate from the situation. I
find these areas of medicine very difficult. I'm not sure what the
right attitude is, but I think there's got to be someone in the
room who's not crumbling. I think if I crumbled they'd probably
think I'd done something wrong, but that's just my suspicious
Presbyterian nature coming to the fore again!

'I think I should stand back'

DR RUSSELL HITCHCOCK, THE MIDLANDS CHEST PHYSICIAN: I have a
number of young patients with cystic fibrosis and I find they
cause me an awful lot of emotional upset at times. I see them

regularly and, of course, as they get worse I see them more and more often, and I get to know their families incredibly well. When it comes to one of them dying that's really quite tough, very upsetting, and it's hard then not to show my emotions, but I do think I should, to some extent, stand back and not get too involved, even though I may feel it.

'Are you going to sob in a corner?'

MR RICHARD DOUGLAS, THE SURGEON FROM SOUTH-WEST ENGLAND: I think you can share a person's grief, but you don't have to break down over it. I think you've got to stay in control if you're doing my sort of job. Because not only the patients, but also the nurses and everybody expect you to be in control at all times and if they see you cracking up over something, well, what's going to happen to you when you're faced with a problem in the operating theatre? Are you going to rip off your gloves and go sob in a corner somewhere? You can't do that as a surgeon.

These four doctors were all concerned that revealing the human side of themselves, through spontaneous displays of emotion, might jeopardise their standing with patients or other colleagues. They felt, as many doctors do, that lack of emotional control implies weakness (and in Mr Cameron's case, guilt), something they could accept in patients but not in themselves. The myth of the heroic super-doctor operates here again, encouraging doctors to appear invulnerable even though they're not. It's a myth which needs to be dispelled because, when taken to extremes, it locks doctors into an image which is helpful neither to their patients nor themselves.

The other reason doctors use to justify their detachment from patients is that emotional involvement might impair their judgement in medical management. Certainly, difficult decisions have to be made in some cases, and a doctor's emotional involvement could make it hard for him to think rationally, but the danger of such an attitude is that it will come to govern the doctor's dealings with all his patients, not just the few in which particularly painful decisions have to be made.

By attempting to suppress any human interaction between himself and his patients, the detached doctor stifles a powerful and therapeutic element of their relationship. Joan Sanders, a 54-year-old lady with breast cancer, had suffered at the hands of a doctor who had behaved in this way:

'I wished I could cry on his shoulder'

Several months after I'd had the breast lump removed and had finished the radiotherapy treatment they did a body scan because I was getting a lot of pain in my back. When I saw the doctor to get the scan result he told me that the cancer had spread and was now in my bones. I couldn't help bursting into tears because I thought that could only mean there was no hope. I was terribly, terribly frightened and wished that I could cry on his shoulder and have him comfort me. But he just sat there, not really saying anything, as I fished around in my pockets trying to find a hankie. Somehow I felt that he didn't really care about me and for weeks afterwards I kept thinking that was why he told me there was no more treatment he could offer.

I met an alarming instance of this rigid professional detachment not in an older, authoritarian doctor, as one might expect, but in Dr Shearing, the young houseman who appeared to take everything in his stride:

'You have think of people like cars'

DR MARK SHEARING: I don't find people dying particularly stressful; I think I've been very upset only once. I try to look at things from a very detached point of view. You have to think of people a bit like cars: they do go wrong, and they do have to come to an end. I think it's very important to have a professional relationship with patients. You either take a liking to them or you don't, as you do with anybody, and that's something you've got to suppress as a doctor because you've got to be fair. You have to treat everybody the same way.

GR: You feel you should suppress any liking for them, as well as any dislike?

DR MARK SHEARING: Oh yes. If you like somebody you mustn't get emotionally attached to them because nice people die as well. You mustn't get upset by that. You've got to treat it as a job, not as part of your life. It must never become that because it's very dangerous.

GR: But ours is a peculiar job in the sense that the 'commodity' with which we work is live human beings who have individual characters. . . .

DR MARK SHEARING: I say, 'So what?' It's a very important commodity, *the* most important commodity – I wouldn't dispute that for one second, but even so, if you're going to be good you have to be careful, you have to be fair. I think the interaction can be directed very much from a detached point of view because you can put on a face which the patient approves of and if you've done that, and the patient is happy, then the interaction has been successful as far as I'm concerned.

I suspect that behind Dr Shearing's cocksure and seemingly insensitive front hid a rather insecure young man, inexperienced at handling dying patients. His efforts to distance himself from patients were aided and abetted by the hospital environment, where inadequate staffing, heavy workloads, and the brevity of most admissions, give doctors and patients little opportunity to get to know one another. It takes real commitment to overcome these obstacles and the only hospital doctors I met who seemed to be doing so with any success were those whose work involved them with many terminally ill patients.

Dr Stuart Menzies was a benign, avuncular man who had worked as a radiotherapist for 31 years. For most of that time he had been a consultant at a district general hospital in the north-east of England where, along with another consultant, he ran a small radiotherapy unit. He was enthusiastic about the successful outcome of much radiotherapy treatment, but was also able to accept the limitations of his specialty and endeavoured to give a caring, personal service both to the patients he could cure and to those he could not.

'I often put my arm around their shoulders'

It can be very frustrating work on occasions because you think you've saved somebody, you know, really got them through the disease, and then it all goes wrong. But on the other hand you can get a great deal of pleasure making life happy and comfortable for somebody even if you don't actually cure them. I think the opportunity to help is what I like about the job. Although I may not be able to cure, I'm sure I can make life better and more tolerable for them and I think that's what appeals to me.

When someone is referred to my clinic we always try and make the first interview a long one so they have the opportunity of asking questions and finding out what's going to happen and why. Because this is a small unit my consultant colleague or I see everyone for their follow-up appointments. That means I can see patients right the way through, hopefully until they get better and need no further treatment, but if we do come to the stage of requiring terminal care then I have quite an input into the hospice over the road so I can also see them through that as well. The personal follow-up makes the job very satisfying.

I often have to repair the damage done by other doctors before I can work with patients. It's not only the surgeons, although they do tend to be a bit brusque, but some of the physicians, and even housemen too. There's an awful bluntness and lack of feeling and forethought about some of these people. They're terrible. I think that we show a certain amount of, well, almost affection for patients. In the clinic I often put my arm around their shoulders or sit and hold hands with them. It's genuine – I don't do it in any pretentious way – and I think they appreciate it because it's very much a personal relationship. But it does drain you a lot. You get very tired.

Another consultant who devoted time to both the physical and emotional aspects of care was Dr Christine Donaldson, the paediatric oncologist caring for children with leukaemia at a teaching hospital in the north of England. While doing her best to grapple with the disease, she also acknowledged the anguish and grief which the parents of her leukaemic patients, and she herself, had to endure, and she was not afraid to share those feelings with the families concerned.

'I'm not concerned about parents seeing me upset'

DR CHRISTINE DONALDSON: I think there's no doubt this is a stressful job, but I think the tension I feel is nothing compared to

183

the tension the parents feel. We try to be as flexible as we can, making sure that they don't spend too long at the hospital, making it easier for them to collect their drugs from the pharmacy, altering out-patient appointments to fit in with Dad's shift work and so on.

GR: Do you ever feel there's any conflict between the emotional side of your nature responding to the tragedy of a child dying and a need to maintain the professional face of a coping doctor?

DR CHRISTINE DONALDSON: Well, I've just had to give up on that score! I try very hard to be rational but I'm not concerned about parents seeing me upset. They know I'm a mum because I talk about our boys, and the dog and the cat, so they know that I exist in a family, and I think that if I do show an emotional side then they see me as a mother probably, not as a doctor. I don't think it does them any harm to see me being emotional. I don't think it destroys any professionalism.

Whether it's a help to them or not depends on how they interpret it, but it seems to have been helpful to at least one of my SHOs funnily enough. We lost a lad of 18 last month whom I'd known since he was 13. I was great pals with him. During his terminal illness he had some cerebral problems and then had a window of lucidity. He was talking to his mum and to me in that little window and I started to cry. I talked to his mum for a while and then went out into the treatment room with the nurse. Then my SHO came in and saw me upset and I said, 'Just let me have my tears and I'll be all right.' Afterwards the SHO said it was good for him to see me as I was because it showed him that I cared.

Dr Donaldson's job involved her in strenuous efforts to cure children of their leukaemia and also in caring for those who were dying because treatment had failed. How did she marry these two sides of her work?

'Part of our job is knowing when to stop'

I think we – I mean paediatric oncologists in the UK – have always prided ourselves on the fact that we don't go on to the bitter end. Part of our job is knowing when to stop, knowing when you're beaten and accepting defeat and helping families make the best of the last few months or weeks. You have to come to terms with failures. I don't actually see them as failures. I prefer to see them as stepping stones to success because you do learn from each child's living disease and death.

Dr Donaldson and Dr Menzies believed that emotional support and medical treatment were equally important components of the care they offered patients. Both worked in relatively small units (although these were in large, busy hospitals) which helped them to provide a personal service to the mutual satisfaction of patients, relatives and the doctors themselves. Knowing patients and their families over a space of months or years encouraged the doctors to look beyond the disease that needed treatment, and see instead a person, a 'whole' person as the clichéd term reminds us, who may well have psychological, spiritual, domestic and financial problems which deserve just as much attention as the physical aspects of their illness.

In many ways GPs should be in an ideal position to provide this kind of 'total' care since they have often known patients and their families for years before the blow of incurable illness strikes, and once the diagnosis is made, they have the opportunity to continue caring for the patient until they die, as well as helping the relatives during their bereavement. Despite these facilitating factors, GPs often find terminal care difficult.

'I find it very taxing'

DR HENRY WINTERTON, THE WEST-COUNTRY GP: I find it extremely hard work, very distressing and emotionally very taxing. If I know the dying person well and am very fond of them it's more taxing. In a way terminal care is emotionally enlarging although it's exhausting. It's rather like training physically. It's exhausting when you run nine miles but it makes you a bit better at running nine miles the next time you have to do it.

'It's more rewarding to care for someone you know'

DR HILARY TAYLOR, THE 34-YEAR-OLD LONDON GP: I haven't had to look after all that many patients dying at home since I started

185

in general practice four years ago, but those that I have cared for have been quite a strain to deal with. Not because they or their families are any trouble – I've found them immensely grateful for the time and attention they receive from the practice – but partly because of the workload that terminal care involves, and partly because of my own emotional response to dying patients and their families.

When patients seem to be nearing the end I try to visit once, twice or even three times a week and they're not just quick in-and-out visits. I feel I should give the family as much time as they want whenever I go, so I'll often be there for half an hour or more. That can be difficult to fit into an already packed day, and sometimes I think the family must be able to tell that I'm in a hurry which is awful. Emotionally, I find it quite distressing at times, because I know the patient and their family well. I'm much more aware of their fears and their sadness than I ever was as a hospital doctor. I didn't know the patients and relatives then, so it was easier to detach myself from them. I think it's much more rewarding to care for someone you know well, but it's much more stressful too.

It was the inadequate care provided for terminally ill people, whether dying at home or in hospital, that prompted the development of the hospice movement led by Dame Cicely Saunders. Her aim was to bring peace and dignity to the dying, by attending to their physical needs, especially pain control, and their mental, emotional and spiritual needs as well. Hospices have now sprung up all over the country: in April 1989 there were 133 in-patient units throughout the UK and Republic of Ireland, and about 260 Home Care Teams helping patients in their own homes. Although the building of hospices has been vital in achieving Dame Cicely's goals, it is the gradual implementation and acceptance of 'hospice philosophy' which is of even greater importance, because the approach it fosters can vastly improve the terminal care given to people dying in hospital and at home too.

Although doctors, nurses and other health professionals work alongside one another in hospitals and in the community, there is often little more than lip service paid to the concept of teamwork. In hospices, however, a team approach is regarded as crucial if the best possible care is to be given to patients. This is not only because there are more minds and more pairs of hands attending to the patients' needs – this could, of course, present problems of its own – but because a united team can provide much-needed support for its individual members, enabling them to give more to the patients in their care.

Dr Ian Kennedy, a thoughtful and sensitive man in his late thirties, had worked in hospital radiotherapy units before moving into the field of hospice care. He told me about the advantages of working in a hospice.

'I was amazed at the team'

One of the things I found in the radiotherapy units was that everyone was pulling in different directions, but when I first came to the hospice I was amazed at how together the team felt, at how the staff's ideas and concerns were sorted through and then actively incorporated into the treatment programme.

I have horrendous memories of when I was working in a hospital and was transfusing blood into a dying man. I felt torn as to whether it was the right thing to do, but the consultant had said I must, and because it seemed then as if my whole career depended on doing what the consultant told me to do, I didn't feel able to disagree with him. And then the sister shouted down the corridor at me, 'I wouldn't thank you for that if he were my father.' Yet if I hadn't transfused him there'd have been another nurse saying, 'So you're letting him die are you?' There was always a conflict of interests amongst the staff over what one should and shouldn't be doing.

Dr Kennedy also described how the hospice approach depends on contributions from all the team members, and explained why he alone could never achieve what the team achieved together.

'It's all done by teamwork'

The whole system in the hospice is so different to hospital. Admissions, for example, are planned very carefully. Patients are met at the door and welcomed by name. When they get to the

ward there'll be someone there to greet them and a hot water
bottle will be warming up the bed. Much more thought goes into
the running of the place so that when patients come here they
feel wanted right from the word go and you're constantly
reminded that it's all done by teamwork. What I do here is only
useful because it's done in the context of a high standard of
nursing, with the social and spiritual back-up we get from our
social workers and chaplain, and with physios who are sensitive
to the needs of the patients. In a sense that's the same in all
hospitals and doctors are fooling themselves if they really believe
that they're the kingpin.

The team approach appears to be noticed and appreciated by
patients. An elderly man at one hospice said:

'A tremendous family set-up'

When I came to the hospice after just a few days I realised
that I was part of a tremendous family set-up. And they are
family. They're family in as much as from the medical staff down
to the cleaners you have a whole family whose sole concern is
caring. And I suppose to be cared for is so unique for me after
so many years of being on my own that I find it so rewarding, so
reassuring, so satisfying. It gives me an inner glow that I haven't
experienced for many years.

Doctors working in a hospice inevitably face the same dilemmas as GPs or those working in hospital, including the vexed
question of how emotionally involved they should, or should
not, let themselves become with dying patients. Dr Kennedy
allowed himself to feel, and express, empathy for patients and
their families while still remaining mindful of the dangers of
over-involvement.

'I feel for them, and with them'

Doctors are led to believe they shouldn't feel emotion. In fact,
I'm not sure that's what we're actually *taught*, but we interpret
what we've been taught as meaning that, because it's actually
quite painful to feel emotion, so we tend to block it off and
say that if we get emotionally involved then we can't be of

professional help to this person. Well, yes, there's some truth in
that. One can't just sit and weep. Being a good doctor involves
being professional and standing away from the emotion of it and
looking at the physical things that need sorting out. But the
danger is that we can become like a lot of modern medicine –
where the emotional side is completely ignored. I think it's
important for me to let some of those emotions come to the
surface at times. It's important for the patient to see that in fact
I do feel for them, and feel with them.

One doctor, who initially trained as a GP but had been in
hospice work for two years when I met him, said this of his
relationships with patients:

'We've put ourselves on that pedestal'

DR PAUL MARKS: This is very much a place for hugging and
holding, for touching and sharing. It took me a long time to learn
that. I think it does help patients to see when we're sad. It's OK
to show emotion. It's a normal response. They don't expect us to
be superhuman.

GR: But we think they expect us to be superhuman, don't we?

DR PAUL MARKS: I suppose so. We've put ourselves on that
pedestal as much as letting them put us up there. It's taken me
two years to find a step-ladder and come down.

If doctors dealing with dying patients on an infrequent basis
find the task stressful, how do staff dealing with them day in
and day out cope? Not by shying away from the enormous
demands on their time and energy, but instead by admitting
their own need for understanding and relaxation away from
work, and for support from colleagues in the hospice team.

'I felt like a chewed-up piece of string'

DR IAN KENNEDY: There are situations one goes into, say where
someone has just come into the hospice who's in great
distress, and a lot of that distress or the emotion inevitably rubs

189

off on to the staff. I can think of an example which happened
recently. The patient was a lady who was very, very frightened of
dying and just nothing was right for her. Every time you touched
her she screamed. It was hard to separate out what was physical
pain, what was mental pain and what was spiritual pain. She
was really too ill to get close to her, to sort it through, and her
family were gravely distressed. So to try and take the history of
her case, and make her comfortable, and be calm, was very
exhausting and at the end of it I just felt like a chewed-up piece
of string. It helped to say to another member of staff, 'That was
bloody. That's how I feel,' and have a cup of tea with them and
take a breather.

As well as this tremendous informal support there's also a
formal set-up in the shape of a weekly ward meeting where the
whole team gets together – chaplain, doctor, nurse, physio,
everybody involved in the care of the patients comes to that –
and difficult problems on the ward are talked about. That's good,
because people can express how they're feeling. And also there
are times when patients are just jolly irritating and it's helpful to
be able to say that.

So hospice doctors have no less stress to contend with than
other medical colleagues, yet they seem to be able to build good
relationships with dying patients and meet needs which are
sometimes not satisfied by GPs and hospital doctors. What do
they think enables them to do this?

'We give people time'

DR IAN KENNEDY: I think one thing that counts is the feeling of
time we try and give people – the feeling of being listened to,
and being heard out, and exploring questions with the family and
patient. One of the great stresses of the hospice is that very often
I *don't* actually have a lot of time. I have to appear calm and
relaxed, with all the time in the world, when in fact there are lots
of things shouting at me wanting to be done. I've had to train
myself not to look at my watch and not to shuffle from foot to
foot, but to take time, sit down and close the door. I make a
point of never talking to people in a corridor. No matter how
little the question is I will always ask if they'd mind sitting down
in the lounge to talk. I ask them if they'd like a cup of tea. They

always say no, but the fact that you've asked is important. They know by your actions that you've got time to talk to them. These sort of skills are necessary not just for dealing with the dying, but for dealing with all patients. They should be part of an undergraduate's training.

Dr John Blackmore, the hospice director, agreed that training for medical students was vitally important in improving care for the dying.

'We rely on what the patient tells us'

I look on it now as a generation problem. I don't really expect, with a few exceptions, to change the way consultants behave. I do expect that we will have changed the way undergraduates think about terminal care, but it will take at least ten years for them to come along the pipeline and end up as consultants.

I think there are three main areas we must teach students. Firstly, they should be introduced to communication skills and human responses. Nowadays there is no excuse for not giving instruction on communication skills because there are superb teaching materials available. Human responses – well, that would give them an outline of the psychological problems in the patient, the family and the doctor when faced with death, loss and bereavement.

Secondly, they need some framework on symptom control. General principles mainly, like the emphasis we put on allowing the patient to decide about the level of pain they want to put up with. We rely enormously on what the patient tells us and that's very different from the rest of medicine which largely relies on doctors making the decisions.

Thirdly, I think they should be quite clear about the enormous advantages of the multi-disciplinary approach. I think one of the sad things I see in the local teaching hospitals is the separation of doctors and nurses, not sharing information.

As well as these three areas, we've got to give undergraduates a sense of the importance of caring for people who've got illnesses that can't be cured, and at the moment they get a low priority with doctors.

Medical education certainly seems to hold the key to improved care for dying patients and their families, but as Dr Blackmore pointed out, the results of better undergraduate teaching will only be discernible when the present generation of medical students have become the next generation of GPs and consultants. In the meantime, doctors must learn a great deal more about themselves and about the roles they live out in their everyday practice, for only by searching behind the professional mask to understand their own human response to incurable illness, can they help patients and families face the sorrow and fear of impending death.

CHAPTER 10

CONCLUSIONS

DOCTOR-PATIENT RELATIONSHIPS are not a cast from a single mould. They vary with the age and personalities of the people involved, and the nature of the problem which brings them together. The relationship is fluid – like that between any two people. Periods of close involvement may be interspersed with spells of infrequent contact; arguments may erupt but blow over with time; enchantment may give way to annoyance, or mistrust to affection, as doctor and patient get to know one another better. The relationship may be fleeting or last a lifetime, but, regardless of its duration, a person's need for help with physical, mental or emotional problems will always form the basis of their dealings with a doctor. Given the nature of the problems at hand, it's hardly surprising that many people rate their relationships with doctors as second only in importance to those with family and friends.

Patients' dissatisfaction with doctors is far more likely to focus on their attitude and behaviour than on their clinical competence. Allegations of an unprofessional manner or attitude on the part of a GP (or his staff) form the largest single cause of complaints to Family Practitioner Committees, and the Medical Advisory Service, which deals with hundreds of queries every month, reports that many of them are from patients who have experienced communication problems either with their GP or with hospital doctors. Evidence like this shows that people believe the way a doctor relates to them is an integral and very important part of the care that he provides. Unfortunately, doctors' priorities may not mirror those of their patients and when needs are left unmet problems are likely to arise.

If pressed, I think most doctors would choose their clinical expertise as the most important part of the medical care they deliver. It is this aspect of medicine which is emphasised to us as students and which many doctors concentrate on improving once they have qualified. In our undergraduate and post-graduate training our competence is assessed not by patients, but by other doctors, and so, as we continue through a lifetime of medical practice, it is the criteria of our colleagues – scientific knowledge, diagnostic skills and technical expertise – by which we judge our own performance. What a patient values in a doctor may be quite different from what the doctor values in himself, and although patients are the 'consumers' we have not yet learned to see ourselves through their eyes.

It seems inevitable that while the medical profession judges its success or failure according to its own value systems, doctors will continue to disappoint many patients, often not for want of trying, but through misdirected efforts. The disparity between doctors and patients may extend beyond their views on the 'good' doctor's qualities; it may include fundamental attitudes towards health as well. Doctors tend to define illness on the basis of symptoms, physical findings and test results; for patients, illness is often a more nebulous problem – with physical aspects inextricably linked to social, psychological and economic ones.

At times the aims of doctor and patient will tally, for example when the problem is something like a straightforward chest infection. The patient's goal is to be rid of the fever and cough which have made him feel low. The doctor arrives at a diagnosis by listening to the patient's history and examining his chest; in all probability, his objectives will then match those of the patient. A course of antibiotics is prescribed in order to eradicate the infection and both doctor and patient feel the 'right thing' has been done.

Doctor and patient may have different priorities and objectives when dealing with other problems, including chronic conditions. With an illness like diabetes the doctor's picture of the disease is based on knowledge of the physiological and biochemical abnormalities it produces, and his aim is to minimise its harmful effects on the body using diet, drugs and other treatments. Preventive measures are important to the doctor for he sees them as a way of controlling the disease, hence his enthusiasm for frequent monitoring of the patient's blood and urine and his insistence on regular attendance at a diabetic clinic.

Although the high blood sugar level may be the doctor's primary concern, the person with diabetes may be far more worried about the effect of the disease on his social life: dictating mealtimes, limiting what he can eat, marking him as 'the odd one out' because of his need for insulin injections. Far from giving the patient a sense of control over his disease, the daily blood or urine tests may make him feel he is at its mercy. Although the doctor is motivated by good intentions for the patient – attempting to minimise long-term complications of the disease – if adhering to a medical regime causes significant difficulties for the diabetic, then one set of problems may simply be substituted by another. The patient may feel that life under medical surveillance is no better than life with the untreated disease, and so his health, in the broadest sense of the word, continues to suffer.

In a situation like this, the doctor's picture of well-being focuses on body biochemistry, while the patient's may revolve around lifestyle and social activities, and I think much of patients' dissatisfaction with doctors reflects this different approach to ill health. For patients, illness means illness as experienced; for doctors it is illness as learned.

A doctor may study in detail the causes, expected symptoms, available treatment and likely progress of a disease but he will rarely have any personal experience of it. Academic learning alone does not encourage a doctor to empathise with patients, and sometimes it is more of a hindrance than a help; the emphasis in textbooks and medical journals on physical aspects of a disease often leaves doctors unaware of the psychological and social consequences it has for patients. But society's respect for the doctor's specialist knowledge endows him with power in medical matters. Because the doctor takes the dominant role in transactions with patients, it is his 'model' of illness which shapes diagnosis and treatment. He may well be sympathetic to the difficulties of coping with a disease, but if people's experience of illness causes them to question the doctor's advice, they may easily be cast in the role of 'difficult' or 'problem' patients. For the doctor's authority to remain unchallenged his model of illness must rule, so patients are continuously coaxed to accept the doctor's point of view.

The dissension between those who treat and those who are

treated is not solely due to the wealth of scientific knowledge that doctors have and that patients do not, although this is usually how doctors explain away the problem. Patients' priorities differ from our own, we reason, because 'they don't understand' – they don't have detailed knowledge about their disease as we do. With some patients this is patently untrue; they read in depth about their illness, and belong to self-help groups where they compare notes with other sufferers and receive up-to-date information from specialists dealing with their condition. Patients like this often have a huge reservoir of knowledge about their disease, but still their ideas and wishes may conflict with the doctor's. Why? Because they are living with the condition and the doctor is not.

Unless a doctor has suffered from a particular illness, the disease, and disease-under-treatment, experience is something he can learn about only from an affected patient. Although the doctor has in-depth knowledge about biological and therapeutic aspects of the condition, and is therefore generally regarded as being the medical 'expert', the patient also has 'specialist' knowledge of his own, incorporating lay concepts and beliefs, and based not on academic learning, but on first-hand experience of the disease and its treatment. Viewed in this light, the relationship between patient and doctor can be seen as one between *two* experts, each bringing a different, but equally valuable, expertise to matters concerning health and sickness. This point is discussed in the book *Meetings Between Experts*:

It is very simplistic to conceive of consultations as meetings between one person who has ideas and the other who does not. The patient entering the consultation brings his own social world with him in the shape of belief and ideas. The doctor, also, has his ideas and theories. A consultation, therefore, can be considered as a meeting between systems of beliefs and ideas. From this point of view several authors have argued that a priority activity for consultations is the task of allowing an exchange or sharing of these systems of belief. . . . Without such a process there can be no certainty that the consultation can be 'successful' and a great risk of talking and acting at cross-purposes.[1]

1. Tuckett, D., Boulton, M., Olson, C., and Williams, A., *Meetings Between Experts*, Tavistock Publications, 1985; p. 12.

The authors' study of over 1,400 consultations between patients and their GPs highlighted several problems which prevented clear communication between the two groups. Of a random sample of 98 patients three-quarters (76 per cent) mentioned specific doubts or questions which they had during the interview but had not mentioned to the doctor. Patients appeared to explain their behaviour in one or more of the following ways:

They thought it was not up to them to ask questions, express doubts or behave as if their view was important; they said they had purposely left queries and doubts till next time when they could be more certain if what they thought was reasonable; they said that they doubted if their doctor could tell them any more at the moment; they said they felt hurried or unable to think about what they were being told or unable to formulate their views in the heat of the moment; they reported they were afraid of being thought less well of by their doctors; they reported that they were afraid of a negative reaction from the doctor. Only a fifth (19 per cent) of those not asking questions gave as a reason that they were not interested in the answer. Only one in ten (nine per cent) of those not expressing a doubt gave fear of the truth as a reason for not doing so.[2]

Similar feelings were reported by parents who took part in the research study which I mentioned in Chapter Six. The paper 'Parents and the GP' describes how

Parents reported difficulties with understanding some of the 'gobbledegook' in which doctors sometimes couched their advice. A number felt too overwhelmed by it to ask for clarification, not necessarily among those from the less articulate sections of the community, but in both middle- and working-class parents, all of whom in the discussion groups had proved themselves able to talk and question with skill. . . . Parents also felt self-conscious about their own language competence. When they felt they could not use such 'complicated' words as the doctor, they reported becoming inhibited and felt unable to explain their worries and concerns fully.[3]

2. Ibid, p. 103.
3. MacAskill, S. G. and MacDonald, M. B., 'Parents and the GP', Occasional Paper, Advertising Research Unit, Department of Marketing, University of Strathclyde, Glasgow, 1982; p. 7.

All these findings clearly show how patients' (or parents') images of a doctor, and of themselves in relationship to that doctor, can hinder their efforts to communicate effectively. Intimidated by their own belief in the superiority of doctors, patients' questions and doubts will often go unvoiced and therefore unanswered. The doctor's image of himself and of patients may well compound the limited communication between them. The wish to maintain his privileged professional status may encourage a doctor to 'look down' on, and explain little to, patients. Even those who have no such motives (at least consciously) may have been trained to adopt a paternalistic attitude to patients, and so may fail to discuss important issues with them. Any doctor, however caring, may be frightened to admit his own ignorance or uncertainty for fear of losing a patient's respect, and so may choose to evade a 'difficult' subject. Issues which increase the doctor's sense of helplessness or emotional involvement may also be avoided, since they threaten the control he expects of himself and his dealings with patients.

Doctors are programmed to behave in this way while still at medical school. To begin with, they are chosen largely on the basis of their academic success, and not for their ability to relate to and communicate with people. The curriculum and examination system they are then exposed to value the retention and recall of factual information above all else. In hospitals, students are quizzed on their knowledge and clinical skills and soon learn that confidence and certainty are much admired by their teachers, but ignorance and doubt cruelly ridiculed. Although medical knowledge is constantly changing, and many of today's 'facts' will become out of date, doctors in training are made to feel uncomfortable with uncertainty and so hide their doubts, first from teachers and peers, and then from patients too. Students watch their superiors deal with patients in a restrained, impassive way and try to modify their own manner to fit the accepted pattern. In so doing, they come to view any emotional response to patients as a sign of weakness which must be disguised at all costs.

The cool professional detachment which patients so often interpret as indifference on the part of doctors is also a consequence of the rigorous scientific training we undergo. Taught to trust only what is rational and explicable in scientific language, we tend to view illness in predominantly physical terms, and ignore or devalue the social, psychological and spiritual elements of health. Able to explore the world first at microscopic, and then at ultramicroscopic level, doctors have sought to understand the workings of both the healthy and diseased body in terms of cellular and molecular biology. Gradually, we have become more concerned with the cell than the self. It seems that our love affair with science has led us further and further into a maze of reductionist pathways from where we find it impossible to see the thinking, feeling human being as a whole.

In the same way that we have dehumanised patients by concentrating disproportionately on their malfunctioning organs or disturbed biochemistry, so we have dehumanised doctoring by trying to stifle the human interaction between ourselves and those we care for. We value the drugs and surgical techniques that we use to tackle medical problems, but pay little heed to the power of our own personalities as an aspect of treatment. Doctors are now beginning to recognise that the appliance of science may produce good washing machines, but that, alone, it cannot create the kind of medical care people want. Viewing patients in a new light will not be enough though; doctors must learn to view themselves in a new light too.

Unfortunately, the British health care system of the late 1980s is hardly conducive to personalised medicine. No one would deny that the National Health Service makes available to everyone routine and emergency medical care including new, sophisticated techniques for investigation and treatment, but drives to increase efficiency and cut costs within hospitals mean that patients are now processed like goods on a conveyor belt. Out-patients endure long waits in clinics for the briefest of appointments; in-patient hospital stays are shorter to increase the through-put of patients; staff shortages amongst nurses and auxiliaries reduce the personal attention they can provide; and overworked hospital doctors have no time or energy to spend talking to patients. In an age where only private medicine guarantees continuity of care from a doctor and unhurried attention from nursing staff, we are in danger of accepting such personalised treatment as a luxury, rather than as the essential part of medical care that it should be.

For some years doctors and nurses have watched the rot set in, becoming increasingly alarmed at the declining quality of care provided for patients. In December 1987 a statement from the presidents of the three senior Royal Colleges (the Physicians, Surgeons, and Obstetricians and Gynaecologists) warned that the NHS was in crisis and called for more funding. A week later, a petition signed by 1,000 consultants and junior doctors, claiming that patients' lives were being endangered, was delivered to Downing Street. In the same month a report from the Policy Studies Institute revealed pessimism and disenchantment amongst doctors, particularly those in the junior ranks. Industrial action by nurses in 1988 further highlighted the declining morale of NHS staff, as well as their concern over falling standards of patient care.

The medical and nursing professions are beginning to speak out, but it's time that the consumers of NHS care also made their feelings clear. In July 1988, when the NHS celebrated its 40th anniversary, a Gallup Poll in the *Daily Telegraph* showed that satisfaction with the Health Service had fallen by 34 per cent since 1956. The paper reported that 'as with many aspects of life, there appears to be a growing element of impersonality in the patient–doctor relationship. Although 60 per cent of the public thought of their doctor as a friend in whom they could confide, 31 per cent thought otherwise. This compares with 79 per cent and 16 per cent in 1956.'[4] Public concern has seemingly grown since the Government's 1989 review of the Health Service, for another Gallup Poll, published in February 1989, revealed that 60 per cent of the population believed the NHS would be in worse shape in ten years' time than it was then.

If people were content with a more impersonal kind of health service, then doctors could be allowed to immerse themselves in science and technology, concentrating solely on the physical aspects of medical care. But people want more than that, as a *Which?* survey published in 1987 clearly showed. Over 2,500

4. *Daily Telegraph*, July 4th 1988; © The *Daily Telegraph* plc, 1988.

adults were asked about their GP's services and 'what mattered most to patients was the way the consultation was carried out – what the doctor's attitude to the patient was, how much the doctor explained about the problem and any medicine, how much time there was for the consultation, and so on.'[5] Time, attention, warmth and understanding are obviously important aspects of treatment for the consumers of NHS care, but they must say so loud and clear before such qualities are squeezed out of the service by relentless government demands for efficiency and economy. The time has come for patients publicly to defend the personalised and humane medical care they value, if they are to prevent it disappearing altogether from the public health sector.

The future could spell doom and gloom with dissatisfaction so evident amongst the medical profession and public. Disgruntled doctors and patients have already taken to blaming one another for some of the problems they experience. If things are to improve we must all grasp the real nature of the health care dilemma, for the conflict to be overcome is not so much one between doctors and patients, but between the science and art of medicine.

Medicine today has been shaped by scientific and technological advances. While such 'progress' has undoubtedly resulted in new, and often life-saving, treatments, it has also introduced a degree of insensitivity into medical care. The demand for bedside diagnoses to be backed up by 'hard' laboratory data concentrates the doctor's mind more on investigations and results than on the patient to whom they pertain. His rigorous scientific training biases the doctor against aspects of illness – social and emotional, for example – which cannot easily be quantified, analysed and dealt with using drugs, surgery or modern technology. The doctor may genuinely have his patient's welfare at heart but with his scientific spectacles firmly in place, the problem he 'sees' may be very different from that which the patient experiences.

If scientific indoctrination produces medical concepts of disease which often bear little relation to patients' experience, should we dispense with science and technology altogether?

5. *Which?*, May 1987; p. 230.

Few would want that, for it would deprive us of benefits accrued from centuries of enquiry into medicine and related fields. What patients seem to want is a doctor capable of utilising his scientific knowledge without it dominating his view of their illness; a doctor whose use of technology will not erode the intimacy between them. Can doctors provide sophisticated medical care with a personal touch? I would like to think so, but if patient-centred medicine really is our goal then the standards set by patients, not by science, should govern the way we practise.

Only with cooperation and communication can we hope to develop more 'rounded' medical care. Cooperation between a doctor and patient implies that both have something to teach and learn; by sharing their priorities, their problems and their goals, they can negotiate care which is truly in the best interests of the individual. Such ideals are not easy to put into practice. To do so, doctors must stop playing God and patients must allow them to relinquish that role. Medical decision-making can then become a dual responsibility, with both sides working to understand the medical problems and personal needs which must be attended to in treatment.

Is such cooperation a pipedream? Thankfully, it would seem not, for the tentative efforts which have already been made to bring doctors and patients together in learning situations have met with considerable success. One example was a symposium held in March 1988, organised chiefly by GPs in Huntingdon, which set out to involve patients and the health profession in a joint educational venture concerned with chronic skin diseases. GPs, consultants, nurses, health visitors, experts in communication skills and a significant number of patients (including members and officers of the Psoriasis Association) were amongst the 150 who attended. Reporting on the symposium Dr Bob Berrington wrote:

On the day, patients played an impressive part as lay teachers of the medical and nursing professions in a mixture of keynote talks and group discussion. If group feedback and audience reaction are reliable indicators, this complete reversal of traditional educational roles worked very well, especially in considering

202

factors which influence quality of life or the value of treatment. . . .

One message which came out of the symposium is that, despite Dennis Potter's *The Singing Detective*, neither the profession nor the public fully understand the physical and emotional problems surrounding chronic skin diseases such as eczema and psoriasis.

It also became clear that patients and their support groups are a major untapped educational resource. In both undergraduate and postgraduate medical and nursing education, much more emphasis should be placed on the quality of patients' lives, particularly in chronic disease. Traditional clinical teaching alone is inadequate for this purpose, and may lead to inappropriate management. Doctors often need to be released from the perceived obligation to cure and, as one speaker said, to show instead 'competence, care and concern'.[6]

Patients have also been recognised as effective teachers in a series of workshops held in Christchurch, New Zealand, designed to help doctors improve their communication skills. Dr John O'Hagan, a consultant physician and Associate Dean for Post-graduate Affairs at Christchurch Clinical School, described the philosophy of the workshops and their outcome:

After our experience in some other seminars, we came to appreciate that the most compelling teachers were the patients themselves, if they were placed in a safe and caring situation where they could give positive and negative feedback to doctors on their communication performance. We [doctors] rarely have the chance to get honest feedback from our customers and we needed to set up a situation where this was possible and fruitful educationally. Furthermore, we discovered that doctors' spouses or other personal partners were often the only ones who would honestly confront issues of communication behaviour with their professional 'other halves'. So we have set up 3-day workshops involving doctors, patients and some doctors' spouses. Initially these have been with family medicine registrars [the equivalent of GP trainees], but twice in the last year we have involved 20 physicians from a range of sub-specialties.

[As part of the workshop] a skilled chairman interviews the

6. Berrington, B., 'Patient Teachers', *Journal of the Royal College of General Practitioners*, 1988; vol. 38, p. 290.

patients for an hour, concentrating on the good and bad aspects of the encounters they have had with their various doctors. The objective is to get the other participants to listen closely to the patients' perspective. [Also included in the workshops are group discussions, role-playing exercises and videos of consultations; the whole experience is intended to] lift the doctor's head beyond the patient to the family and other important forces in the patient's life and illness. Further, to get the doctor to appreciate all the influences focusing on his own behaviour, e.g. his partner, family, mentors etc., so he can understand 'why I behave in this way'.

This has been a most powerful influence for change and clearly had a tremendous effect on most participants, all of whom became involved. Our evaluation of these workshops indicates that they have been enjoyed and considered very helpful.[7]

Both the East Anglian and New Zealand projects have shown that patients can help modify doctors' attitudes and aims, and so encourage them to provide care which is sensitive to the individual's needs. Faced with a profession which is often imperious and reactionary this is a difficult role for patients to take on, but one which could help revolutionise medical care. More and more dissatisfied patients are bringing complaints against their doctors, or turning to alternative practitioners for help, but neither move will change the profession which has disappointed them. Helping to re-educate doctors might though, so patient groups must seize this opportunity to influence prevailing medical ideas and opinions.

For many doctors, accustomed to a hierarchy in which patients are subservient, change is difficult, if not impossible. Those who have practised medicine for many years may be so entrenched in their view of patients and of disease that no amount of encouragement will persuade them to adopt a new, more equal partnership with those to whom they give medical care. Such rigidity often stems from fear (patients may likewise cling to familiar, but restrictive, relationships with doctors because adopting a new role seems too threatening) and, since old habits die hard, there is an urgent need to help medical students,

7. Personal communication to GR from Dr John O'Hagan, 26th October 1988.

from the moment they start their training, to be flexible in their attitude towards both doctor and patient roles.

Communication, the second key to better medical care, is also difficult for many patients and doctors. Few people are skilled communicators, even with their family and friends and, given the anxiety that most feel when consulting a doctor, it's not surprising that they often fail to convey thoughts, feelings and relevant information. The passive role that patients may feel obliged to adopt in medical encounters can only further inhibit their attempts to communicate effectively. Only when people feel that their beliefs and opinions are valued by doctors will they be able to talk and question more openly, and even then they are likely to need certain skills to help them do so.

Greater emphasis on human biology, disease, and health issues in schools would give everyone a grounding in basic medical concepts which would make it easier for them to communicate with doctors. For now, a change in general attitudes towards doctor and patient roles would be sufficient to give many people the 'permission' they need to voice previously hidden ideas during consultations. Others will require more specific help, such as that provided in assertiveness training groups. Still more will want practical guidance (perhaps in leaflet, book or video form) on how to get ideas, information, questions and doubts across to their doctor and ensure that the explanations and instructions they receive make sense. Aids like these have so far been tried with only a few patients, but they have proved very useful and obviously have the potential to help many more people communicate successfully with doctors.

As part of their research into sharing ideas in medical consultations, the authors of *Meetings Between Experts* produced a pamphlet for patients entitled 'Speak for Yourself: A Guide to Asking Questions of Your Doctor'. The pamphlet explained why it is important for patients to voice their questions, and discussed ways in which they could best get information and ideas across to the doctor. It included advice to help patients make sure they understood what they had been told and tackle any difficulties they experienced in the consultation. Although doctors taking part in the pamphlet project had some initial doubts about it, in the event they agreed thus:

Only one of their expressed fears had proved accurate. Patients from minority ethnic groups [to whom no special concessions were made in the pamphlet] seemed to find the experience mystifying. Other patients read the pamphlet, appreciated it, used it to jot down and organise their thoughts, and found it clear and understandable. They did not bring the feared 'shopping lists' [of problems] and in some cases, apparently as a direct result of the pamphlet, seemed to have opened up areas of discussion with their doctors which they had clearly held back in the past. In this way they allowed their doctors to provide them with important and much-needed information.[8]

A pamphlet similar to this one (entitled 'Talking to your Doctor') has been produced by the Medical Advisory Service (10 Barley Mow Passage, London W4 4PH) and is available free to members of the public.

Learning communication skills is not just a job for patients, but for doctors too. It seems almost inconceivable that professionals who spend their lives dealing with people should receive no training in how to do so, but until recently the important business of talking to patients was ignored in medical school curricula. It was assumed that good communication was a heaven-sent, inborn skill which all medical students possessed. Hundreds of years' experience in which both doctors and patients have learnt for themselves the falsity of this notion did not prevent the myth surviving. Only recently has the medical profession begun to acknowledge the rumblings of discontent within its ranks and amongst patients, and to recognise the importance of communication skills teaching for would-be doctors.

Although the General Medical Council's 1980 Recommendations on Basic Medical Education[9] stated that on graduation, a

---

8. Tuckett, D., Boulton, M., Olson, C., and Williams, A., *Meetings Between Experts*, Tavistock Publications, 1985; p. 193.
9. Recommendations promulgated by the General Medical Council's Education Committee, February 1980.

medical student should be able 'to communicate effectively and sensitively with patients and their relatives', a Working Party Report[10] in 1987 admitted that 'this recommendation is not strong enough to encourage the proper development of teaching [in communication skills].' The majority of medical schools have been slow to follow the GMC's 1980 advice but the results of my own 1988 survey on communication skills teaching were moderately encouraging. Twenty-four of the 27 medical schools in the United Kingdom replied and of these, one provided no communication-skills teaching at all, 11 gave less than 10 hours to the subject, 9 provided between 10 and 20 hours, and 3 gave more than 20 hours of teaching to their students. Fifteen of the schools had definite plans to increase the amount of time devoted to communication skills teaching in the near future but it is interesting to note that in only two medical schools is there any attempt formally to assess students' communication skills in their final examinations.

There is obviously a long way to go before communication skills teaching is given the priority it deserves in medical school curricula, but demands for more time to be devoted to it are increasing – from social science, education and communication skills experts, from patient associations and from a small but growing number of doctors. Representatives from all these groups were among more than a hundred people who attended Britain's first national conference on communication in medicine, held in Cambridge in July 1988. For three days participants discussed issues relating to communication between patients and health professionals, and in particular, ways of improving the communication skills of medical students and doctors.

Excitement and frustration were both evident at the conference, for although those of us participating were enthusiastic about the benefits of communication skills teaching, we also acknowledged the many barriers which have to be overcome before it can become a significant part of doctors' training. Not only have most medical schools yet to be convinced that communication is as important a part of student learning as, say,

10. 'The Teaching of Behavioural Sciences, Community Medicine and General Practice in Basic Medical Education', Report of a Working Party of the General Medical Council's Education Committee, March 1987.

anatomy or physiology, but they must also understand the way in which these skills need to be taught. Boxed into one segment of the curriculum, particularly during the first two years when most medical students have no contact with patients, communication skills can easily be seen by the students as something unrelated to the 'real' medicine they learn on the wards. Sometimes the topic is dealt with during their general practice or psychiatry training and then students are in danger of thinking that communication is important only in these two areas of medical practice. To avoid these pitfalls, good communication with patients must be emphasised throughout the whole medical course, and sufficient time and guidance provided to help students achieve this.

A bold call for change in medical education was heard in August 1988 when an international gathering of doctors met in Edinburgh for a five-day conference and proposed what the *Independent* called a 'world revolution in medical training'. The conference ended with a declaration which questions the existing priorities of medical schools throughout the world and points out that 'scientific research continues to bring rich rewards; but man needs more than science alone, and it is the health needs of the human race as a whole, and of the whole person, that medical educators must affirm.' Most of the 84 recommendations made by the conference delegates involve changes in the way medical schools train students, and an institute has been set up in Edinburgh to help implement the reforms suggested in the conference declaration.

It is an exciting time for anyone concerned about the personal aspect of medical care, for if the character of medical education changes dramatically, then the kind of doctors it produces should change dramatically too. The myths which have for so long portrayed doctors as omniscient, superhuman beings will, I hope, finally be put to rest, relieving those of us in the profession from the burden of trying to live up to the image, and liberating patients from their enforced subjugation in health care matters.

The aim of the radical reforms which I and many others look forward to is not to demote doctors or make them redundant – I, for one, would be out of a job if that was our long-term goal! Nor are we trying to force patients to deal with medical responsibilities that they do not want, or feel able, to cope with.

208

My hope is rather to demolish barriers resulting from fear and ignorance on the part of both the medical profession and the public, and in their place build more flexibility into the way patients and doctors relate to one another.

Doctors must admit to themselves, their colleagues and their patients that they are human. The thoughts and feelings expressed by doctors throughout this book show that they are, but many of their comments also reveal how they have become trapped in a role which makes it impossible for them to confess their weaknesses either to themselves or to others. Many are frightened to drop the façade of rock-like certainty and confidence for fear that their professional influence will disappear along with it. Such fears are largely unfounded, for doctors have knowledge and skills that will always be valued by the public, and it is only patients' timidity, not their affection and respect, that will be diminished by shedding the cloak of mystique which still enshrouds the profession. By becoming less intimidating doctors can improve communication with their patients and so ensure greater mutual understanding, more appropriate treatment, increased compliance on the patient's part and, as a result of all these, a more successful outcome to medical care.

If the medical profession is also to adopt new attitudes towards patients, those patients must be willing to accept the human side, flaws and all, of the doctors who look after them. Some people will feel more ambivalent about doing so than they care to admit. It is one thing to appreciate your doctor's endearing human qualities, like his honesty and warmth, but quite another to accept his tiredness, fallibility and doubts. Yet an equal partnership entails give and take on both sides, so while it is only right that people should be given more say in the management of their medical problems, in order to do so they may have to shoulder some of the uncertainties and anxieties which doctors have previously carried alone.

Dispelling the medical myths which have gone unchallenged for so long may not be a comfortable process for either doctors or patients, but the long-term benefits for us all could be enormous. Real doctors are undoubtedly less glamorous, heroic and tyrannical than their mythical counterparts; we are also more human, and we need to acknowledge that as a strength, not a weakness. All of us, doctors and patients alike, would do well to remember George Bernard Shaw's advice: 'Make it compulsory for a doctor using a brass plate to have inscribed on it, in addition to the letters indicating his qualifications, the words "Remember that I too am mortal".'

INDEX